ELIZABETH AND PHILIP

Our Heiress and her Consort

ELIZABETH

AND

PHILIP

OUR HEIRESS AND HER CONSORT

An authentic sketch of H.R.H. the
Princess Elizabeth and Lieutenant
Philip Mountbatten, R.N.

by

LOUIS WULFF

M.V.O.

(*Author of "Queen of To-morrow"*)

London

SAMPSON LOW, MARSTON & CO., LTD.

Contents

CHAPTER   PAGE

I.   Royal Romance   7

II.   Philip the Fair   19

III.   Marriage and the Constitution   29

IV.   Engagement Days   37

V.   Family Background   47

VI.   Princess Elizabeth To-day   51

Acknowledgments

Thanks are due to P. K. Hodgson, C.M.G., C.V.O., O.B.E., for his courtesy in lending some pictures.

Acknowledgments are due to the following for their help in illustrating this book:

P.A. Reuters—Photos.

The Scotsman.

The Associated Press Ltd.

The London Electrotype Agency Ltd.

Photo Illustrations, Scotland.

Graphic Photo Union.

The Times.

Central Press Photos Ltd.

Fox Photos Ltd.

MADE AND PRINTED IN GREAT BRITAIN BY PURNELL AND SONS LTD.,
PAULTON (SOMERSET) AND LONDON

Author's Foreword

A FAMILY on the Throne, says Bagehot, is an interesting idea. It brings down the pride of sovereignty to the level of petty life.

In 1872, when the great constitutional authority wrote those words, the conception of Royalty was of something much more remote and aloof from everyday affairs than it is to-day when the British monarchy draws part of its greatest strength from its family associations. We speak of the British Commonwealth as a family of nations: and at its head there is a family on whom all eyes are turned as the proto-type and example of what family life should be. The foundations of the nation's glory are laid in the homes of the people, declared King George V; and turning his words slightly we may say with equal truth that the glory of the monarchy is in the home of the King. Nowhere was this more clearly demonstrated than in South Africa during the Royal tour. What impressed the home- and family-loving South Africans, especially those of Boer descent, most about their Royal visitors was the family party atmosphere of the Royal tour. Instead of a host of courtiers with high-sounding titles, the King and Queen brought their two daughters with them; and the Princesses went everywhere with their parents. That impression of the sovereign head of the Empire as the centre of a happy, united family did more than anything else to win the hearts of the Afrikaners, and so set the seal of success on the whole tour.

Now Princess Elizabeth is to be married with all the prospects of a happy family life of her own before her. The whole nation and the Empire at large join in wishing well to her and to Lieutenant Philip Mountbatten, the man of her choice.

Edinburgh and East Horsley,   L.W.
    July 1947.

Court Circular
Buckingham Palace July 9th

It is with the greatest pleasure that The King and Queen announce the betrothal of their dearly beloved daughter The Princess Elizabeth to Lieutenant Philip Mountbatten, R.N., son of the late Prince Andrew of Greece and Princess Andrew (Princess Alice of Battenberg), to which union The King has gladly given his consent.

How the news was given to the world

CHAPTER ONE

Royal Romance

IT WAS on the night of Wednesday, 9th July, that the Court Circular, issued from Buckingham Palace, contained this important passage:

"It is with the greatest pleasure that The King and Queen announce the betrothal of their dearly beloved daughter, The Princess Elizabeth, to Lieutenant Philip Mountbatten, R.N., son of the late Prince Andrew of Greece and Princess Andrew (Princess Alice of Battenberg), to which union The King has gladly given his consent."

The rest of the Court Circular that night was filled with an account of the reception by the King of four Indian Princes, the presentation of Letters of Credence by the new Siamese Ambassador, and the attendance of the Royal Family at the International Horse Show at the White City.

Simultaneously, the news was released in every capital of the Empire. It was flashed across the Atlantic, where it was "Page One" news from coast to coast in the United States. It was the official confirmation of news that the whole world had guessed was coming, and in newspaper offices, columns about the Princess and her fiancé, prepared long before, leaders on the Royal engagement, and agency photographs of the young couple, were rushed to the compositors to take the place of other news, hastily scrapped. The news "broke" at seven p.m., Double British Summer Time. But Fleet Street was not taken entirely unawares. There had, at the very last, been a "leak", and, as a result of a chance conversation in a bar at Athens, confirmed by a direct telephone call to Lieutenant Mountbatten, one London morning paper was able to state in its edition dated 9th July that the engagement would be officially announced "within two days". From Buckingham Palace, whence had previously come nothing but denials, there was now issued a statement that "The King has not yet authorised any statement about Princess Elizabeth. When he does so, it will be made through the usual channels." That was enough for Fleet Street. The engagement was "on" and that Wednesday was a day of intense activity, as reporters and photographers waited outside the Palace gates, followed the Royal Family party (without Philip) to the International Horse Show at White City, hurried down to Corsham, where Mountbatten was stationed, to interview any and every one who had anything to say about him.

Elaborate and strict precautions had been taken by the Palace authorities to prevent premature disclosure of the news in London. Only a very small number of Household officials were in the secret, and security measures went even as far as having the announcement typed separately from the rest of the Court Circular on plain paper instead of, as usual, on the official Palace paper headed with the Royal Crown. All these precautions, which succeeded completely as far as London was concerned, were taken not with a view to hiding anything from the public, but simply to make absolutely sure that this, the most important piece of "domestic" news since the Accession, should be given to the whole Empire at the same time.

A smiling greeting in South Africa

The Court Circular, issued daily from Buckingham Palace or wherever else the King and Queen are in official residence, is usually a somewhat dull record of the official activities of Their Majesties and the Princesses. It was made the vehicle for the engagement announcement because it is the only channel available to the Sovereign for communicating intelligence directly to his people: and the engagement of his daughter was a matter personal to the King, and not to be dealt with by such remote, impersonal and formal means as a message to the House of Commons, read by the Prime Minister. The Court Circular has, indeed, contained the announcements of every birth, engagement, marriage, and death in the British Royal Family for more than a hundred years.

That was the culmination of the engagement story.

Its beginnings go a long way back, to the days when Princess Elizabeth was little more than nineteen years of age. In September, 1945, a report emanating from Monarchist circles in Athens hinted that an alliance was contemplated between Elizabeth of England and Philip of Greece. At that time, it is certain that no engagement was planned. Speculation about whom Princess Elizabeth would marry was rife all over the world, in foreign capitals and the Chanceries of certain Embassies where a false political importance was attached to the affair, in the drawing-rooms of Mayfair, where elderly ladies consulted copies of the Almanach de Gotha, the record of European Royalty and nobility, to search out the non-Roman Catholic Princes of the right age who might be considered suitable suitors for the Princess's hand, and in London clubs and restaurants where members of the Princess's own circle of friends were to be met. All sorts of names were put forward, and it was enough for any eligible young men to be seen two or three times running in her company for another engagement rumour to be put into circulation, and often, on the other side of the Atlantic, where interest in the Princess is always intense, into print.

Very few people can point with any certainty to any one day and identify it as the day they fell in love. None of their friends, and probably neither the Princess nor Philip themselves, could determine when their friendship turned to affection and love. At the time when the rumours started, they had been friends for several years, and theirs was a growing and deepening friendship, which a frequent and uninterrupted correspondence throughout the war had done much to strengthen. When they first met is a little difficult to discover. Philip as a young boy spent a lot of his time at Brook House, the Mountbatten's home in Park Lane, and both Princess Elizabeth and Princess Margaret were frequent visitors there at parties given for the Mountbatten daughters, Patricia (now Lady Brabourne) and Pamela.

It seems likely that the two must have met in those days, but Lieutenant Mountbatten's first recollection of meeting the girl who was to be his wife was at the Coronation of the King and Queen on 12th May, 1937, when he was a schoolboy guest at the festivities.

There is no record that the two were drawn to each other on that occasion, and a long interval of two years and two months elapsed before they met again, this time at the Royal Naval College, Dartmouth, where Philip was enrolled as a cadet. After reviewing the Reserve Fleet in Weymouth Bay, the King and Queen, with their daughters, went on to Dartmouth, where the King had himself once been a cadet, and, after an inspection of the College and its inhabitants, took tea with the Commanding Officer, Captain F. H. G. Dalrymple-Hamilton. Cadet Prince Philip, as a distant relative of the Royal visitors, was selected to be present at the tea party. He and the Princess, not quite five years his junior, seemed to find

A family talk in Natal National Park

much to talk about, and it was Philip who proudly showed the Princess round the College, pointing out various treasures, explaining to her College customs. That evening, Philip, with a few other cadets, dined aboard the Royal Yacht. The war came, sending Princess Elizabeth to a long country sojourn first at Balmoral, then at Windsor, while Philip triumphantly finished his course at Dartmouth and emerged a fully-fledged midshipman, R.N., to be sent off to the Mediterranean. From his ship in the "Med." letters went to Balmoral, and from the Princess's wartime home answers went back. On leave in January, 1940, Prince Philip was entertained by the King and Queen, and went with them on a surprise visit to His Majesty's Theatre, where they saw a musical show, *Funny Side Up*. At that time, of course, Princess Elizabeth, not quite fourteen, was not considered old enough to go to theatre parties, and she remained at home at Windsor Castle, where the Royal sisters had been brought from Scotland for the first Christmas of the war.

Midshipman Philip went back to his ship, and did not see London again for many a long month. But the correspondence, we may be sure, continued, for Princess Elizabeth, like her great-great-grandmother, Queen Victoria, is a great letter-writer, and to have someone on active service as a correspondent was a matter of pride for any girl. When next home leave came round, Prince Philip was invited to stay at Windsor Castle. There, the two saw much of each other, and went long walks together in the Great Park. After that, Windsor Castle was open to Prince Philip whenever he had leave.

When Princess Elizabeth and Princess Margaret were producing their Christmas pantomime one year, Philip was a guest in the Castle, and, like everyone else, he was invited to see the show by the energetic and determined Royal producers. Since he had, as Princess Elizabeth knew, played several times in school productions of Shakespeare with some success, she felt he would appreciate the efforts of her company. It was in 1943, and the Princesses' production was *Aladdin*. Philip, now a lieutenant, sat in the front row of the "stalls" in the Waterloo Chamber with the King and Queen and other members of the Royal Family to watch the show. That was the first time that many of those in the audience had seen him, and it was on that December day that talk about the two really began. Philip, it was noticed, went to the tea-party at which Princess Elizabeth each year entertained members of the cast and others who had helped with the show, and some of the wives of Windsor drew significant (and at the time quite erroneous) conclusions.

Twenty-four years ago, in a wood on her father's estate at St. Paul's Walden Bury, the Queen, then Lady Elizabeth Bowes-Lyon, was asked by the then Duke of York to marry him. Three days later, the announcement of their engagement, couched in the same phrases as that of Princess Elizabeth and Lieutenant Mountbatten, was made in the Court Circular. That much is on record. But there is no indication of when or where the Princess and Philip became betrothed. None of their friends know the date. It is one of the secrets they share with no one else.

Among their friends, their eventual engagement was an accepted thing for a full year before the announcement, but a daughter of the Royal House, even if she is of full age, cannot become engaged without the consent of the Sovereign, and like any father and mother, the King and Queen wanted their daughter to be absolutely sure before she engaged herself.

It was in the romantic setting of the Highlands, amid the great mountains and wide moors that stretch around Balmoral Castle, the King's home in Scotland, that the Princess and Philip really decided they were in love and would marry. In August, 1946, a fair-haired, tall young man in well-fitting sports clothes went out with the King and other guns on the "Glorious Twelfth" for the opening of the grouse shooting. The day's bag was a fair one, and Philip contributed his share to the many brace that were taken back to the Castle. It was his first appearance at Balmoral, where he had been invited by the King and Queen to stay for a few weeks, and among the ghillies and keepers the news that "Philip's here" spread quickly. Princess Elizabeth holds a place of her own in the hearts of the proud and independent men who tend the King's Scottish estates, a place she has won by her personal charm, by her keenness and ability at the difficult and uncomfortable sport of deer stalking, and by her very pronounced love of Deeside, its river and its mountains. So when they found that this year her eyes seemed even brighter, her smile even readier, her happiness more infectious, because of the presence of the young naval gentleman, there was nothing too much that a ghillie or a keeper could do for Philip. And, as anyone who has spent a shooting or a fishing holiday in the Highlands knows, to establish that happy relationship with the men who know the forests and the streams is to ensure a good holiday, and at the same time to be paid a considerable compliment, for the deep hearts of the ghillies are not easy to win.

Philip won the ghillies over completely a few days later. When he shot two fine stags on his first day's stalking, they decided he was a "real man". And shooting deer after several hours' arduous and careful climbing in the mountains is not the easy business it may seem from the comfort of an arm-chair. It is a real test of stamina and nerve.

Princess Elizabeth, herself a proven stalker who shot her first stag in 1942 and her first Royal, or stag with twelve pointer antlers, in 1945, was delighted at Philip's success.

Prince Philip escorts the Royal Family: at the wedding of the Hon. Patricia Mountbatten

For the rest of his stay, Philip went out shooting or stalking every day, and though, by tradition, the ladies do not accompany the guns on the moors, nor is deer stalking a sport calculated to afford many romantic opportunities, the mutual affection and regard between the Princess and Philip continued to increase, until by the time he left Balmoral, on September 13, it was taken for granted that an engagement would, sooner or later, be announced. Many in the highest Court circles believe that it was during this stay at Balmoral that Prince Philip (as he still was) first asked the King for the hand of his daughter, and that the King advised the young people to wait for six months to see if their minds would change.

This suggestion would explain many things which occurred between that visit and the announcement of their engagement ten months later. It was in September, 1946, that the first really definite statement was published in a British newspaper that a marriage between Elizabeth and Philip was forthcoming. At the same time it was stated that denials might be expected. The latter part of the story was proved right immediately, for from Balmoral came this statement by Sir Alan Lascelles, Private Secretary to the King: "Princess Elizabeth is not engaged to be married. The report published is incorrect." Several points about this denial were of interest. First, it is extremely rare for the King's Private Secretary to go on record with a denial of a newspaper story, a fact which in itself lent importance to the story. Secondly, the Foreign Office had taken the report seriously enough to get in touch with Balmoral about it. And, thirdly, its terms, categorical enough, did not entirely dispose of the newspaper statement which was that friends of the couple were no longer discussing whether they would become engaged, but when the engagement would be announced. This was very proper, for no one can deny an event which may take place in the future, yet it was perfectly true that at that time there was no engagement, whatever understanding there may have been between the young people, since the King had not yet given his consent.

That winter, the Princess and Prince Philip were seen about a good deal together, at the weddings of friends, at theatre parties in the West End, and at private dances and parties. Earlier in the year, Princess Elizabeth had been a bridesmaid at the wedding of her Lady-in-Waiting and friend, the Hon. Mrs. Vicary Gibbs, to the Hon. Andrew Elphinstone, the Princess's first cousin, and Prince Philip was among the guests, with his cousin, the late King George II of the Hellenes. On October 26, in the delightful setting of the ancient Abbey of Romsey, in the heart of the New Forest, another friend of the Princess's was married, the Hon. Patricia Mountbatten, elder daughter of Viscount and Viscountess Mountbatten of Burma. Her bridegroom was Lord Brabourne, who had been A.D.C. to her father in Burma. Again, the Princess was a bridesmaid, and this time Philip was an usher. On neither of these occasions, nor at the theatre—at the Aldwych, where they saw *The Hasty Heart*, at the Hippodrome, where they saw *Perchance to Dream*—was there anything to show that the Princess and her Prince were more than just friends. At the Mountbatten wedding, Prince Philip squired Princess Elizabeth with no more marked attention than he showed to other members of the party. But at private dances, when Prince Philip could get leave to be present, driving the hundred miles up from Corsham in well under three hours in his sports car, the two danced nearly every dance together, and rumours of the coming engagement grew stronger and stronger. Several times the Palace authorities were moved to further denials, which took the form of reference to the statement made by Sir Alan Lascelles, "which still holds good". Back in 1945, when Philip came home from the sea complete with a beard it was, their friends averred, Princess Elizabeth who issued orders for him to shave it off.

When Princess Elizabeth left with her parents for South Africa, many people expected to see Philip, still then a Prince of Greece and Denmark, on the platform. But to the disappointment of the photographers, he was not to be seen. Actually, he and Elizabeth had said their good-byes in private some days before. Aboard H.M.S. *Vanguard*, the battleship which took the Royal party to South Africa, rumour followed,

Romsey Abbey "news reel" . . .

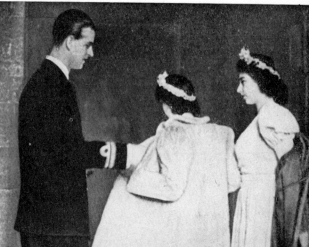

and the present writer, accompanying them as Reuter's correspondent, had more than one enquiry by radio to ascertain if Prince Philip was aboard. He was not. Instead, he was at Corsham, patiently taking his Petty Officers through their courses, waiting till his Princess should return to go again as suitor to her father. Throughout the South African tour, the Princess and Philip maintained a steady correspondence, writing to each other several times a week, and on the Princess's twenty-first birthday in Capetown, one of the very first messages she opened was a telegram of good wishes sent her by Philip, to which she replied in the cipher specially arranged for private Royal messages.

That day was another chosen by rumour as the date for the official engagement, and suggestions that Philip had flown out secretly to the Cape, to spring up like a jack-in-the-box at the Princess's coming-of-age party, were followed by a widely published statement that the King would announce his daughter's engagement on her birthday. This at once drew an authoritative denial from the Royal train, the last denial, as it turned out, before the engagement.

Back home from Africa, the Princess was still followed by rumours. When the Royal party left Waterloo on the morning of May 12 to drive in State to Buckingham Palace, one Press photographer was furious at missing the picture of a lifetime. He had, he declared, seen Lieutenant Mountbatten riding in the last of the four Royal landaus, but had been unable to obtain a picture. He need not have worried. "Lieutenant Mountbatten" was in fact Lieutenant Commander Peter Ashmore, naval equerry to the King, who had been with the party all through the African tour.

Lieutenant Philip was present on another occasion of some importance, the Royal Family luncheon party at Buckingham Palace on May 26, in honour of Queen Mary's eightieth birthday. By that time, members of the Royal Family knew that the engagement was settled in everything but name, and it must have been a great and abiding pleasure to Her Majesty, on her eightieth birthday, to see her beloved granddaughter happy with the man she loves.

From the Palace, Mountbatten went back to duty at Corsham, and now new rumours began to circulate. Tired, apparently, of waiting for the betrothal announcement which did not come, gossips began to put about stories that there was a break-off between the couple. This totally untrue tale even found its way into print in the United States. It had its origin in the fact that deliberately the Princess and her Lieutenant had abstained from public appearances together, a course made the easier by reason of duties which kept Mountbatten at Corsham. This was why he was not, as he had been the previous year, in the Windsor Castle house party for Ascot Week. But he was present, though few outside the Castle knew it at the time, at the dance which Their Majesties gave on the evening of the last day's racing. In the Red Drawing-Room

. . . Prince Philip squires the Royal bridesmaids

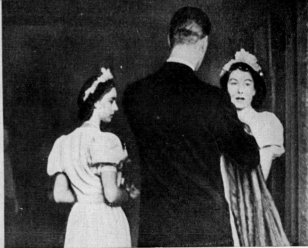

of Windsor Castle a small party of about one hundred young folk, all of them close friends of the young pair, danced to music from a band which went on playing until well after three in the morning, and Princess Elizabeth and Philip missed scarcely one dance together. It was really a pre-engagement party, for the announcement came only a fortnight later. When she heard of the newest rumours, the Princess dismissed them, as she had the earlier ones of her premature engagement, with a smile, a smile that delighted senior members of the Royal Household, for it showed clearly that Princess Elizabeth has too strong a character to allow idle gossip or newspaper reports to affect her or to interfere with her happiness, a most valuable outlook for anyone whose life and actions are constantly in the public eye.

The best answer to the oft-repeated question whether this Royal romance between the Princess who is heiress to the greatest throne in the world and the Royal-born young man who threw away his titles and rank to become one of her father's subjects, is a

In "Service rig" at sea :
Princess Elizabeth wears a "Vanguard" ribbon

real love match or not, is to watch the Princess and Philip when they are dancing together. Each is a good dancer with any partner, but when they are dancing with each other there is something in the rhythm of their steps, something in the way they look at each other, that tells their story. They seem—and are—completely happy in each other's company. When they are not on the dance floor, when they are walking, not arm in arm, for that is something that Royalty does not do in public, but side by side at some official visit the Princess is making, it is easy to see their affection, which shows itself in a hundred different ways. During the Scottish tour, for instance, when Mountbatten first appeared in company with the Royal party, while the packed throngs were cheering the Royal visitors as they walked slowly round the crowded square of Kelso, there was one small person who was not enjoying it in the least, a baby in its mother's arms, crying with a passionate conviction that this Royal occasion was not in his line at all. Philip, noticing the unwilling spectator, drew Princess Elizabeth's attention to him, touching her arm and whispering a comment to her that brought a smile to her lips. Again, in the formality and dignity of the proceedings at Edinburgh's Usher Hall, where Lord Provost Sir John Falconer had just made the Princess a Free Burgess of the city, Mountbatten struck a charming human note. He watched closely as the Princess made her speech. When she finished and resumed her seat, at once her fiancé, forgetful that there was an attentive lady-in-waiting behind, leaned forward and put out his hands to relieve the Princess of her manuscript. At an Edinburgh Service Club, where the Princess was asked to sign the Visitors' Book, there was, by an oversight, no pen for her use. Immediately, Philip produced a fountain-pen from his pocket and handed it to her—receiving it back a few moments later to sign his own name for the first time underneath hers. Small incidents as these are, they show that spontaneous attentiveness that springs from true affection.

Dancing is but one of the many tastes the Princess and Philip share in common. Another is the theatre. Each is fond of seeing any piece of the theatre, from a serious play to a musical comedy, and Philip has, like the Princess, a love of music. He is not so good a pianist as she, and has not taken part in the madrigal singing by a choir of some thirty-three which the Princess arranges every Thursday evening at the Palace. Reading is another interest they have in common, and their literary tastes are much the same, though their serious reading has necessarily hitherto been on diverse lines, the Princess concentrating on such studies as the British constitution, and constitutional history, while Mountbatten has read naval strategy and history, the lives of famous naval commanders, the accounts of famous naval battles. But he has not confined his reading exclusively to Navy matters. Economics, modern European and world history, and the development of political and national movements have been among his special studies.

Another of the mutual interests that bind the two is a love of the outdoors. Princess Elizabeth is rarely happier than when she is walking or riding in the country, far away from crowds, and Lieutenant Mountbatten has all the sailor's traditional love for the green quiet of the English countryside.

One more story of their stay in Scotland shows that Lieutenant Mountbatten, like other young men in love, will do much for his lady. At the big dance at the Edinburgh Assembly Rooms on the night of their arrival, the first public dance they had attended together, the opening dance was, not unexpectedly, a double eightsome reel. Now, Princess Elizabeth is a real expert at the Scottish dances, which she first learned as a little girl at Balmoral from King George V's piper, Pipe Major Forsyth. Mountbatten is not. For the first dance, therefore, he stood at the side, watching the Princess partnered

A morning walk on Table Mountain

by a young Scotch expert. Two days later, there was another dance at the Assembly Rooms, this time the Highland Brigade Ball, organised by the six Highland Regiments. Again, the first dance was a reel, with six sets, one from each regiment. This time the Princess, dancing as Colonel-in-Chief of the Regiment, in the Argyll and Sutherland Highlanders set, was partnered by Lieutenant Mountbatten. And he scarcely put a foot wrong. With that thoroughness that is a family characteristic of the Mountbattens, he had spent all his spare time in the interval between the two dances taking lessons in the reel steps from Princess Elizabeth and from Pipe Major MacDonald, late of the Scots Guards, now Piper to the King.

Not very long ago, Royal marriages were arranged with or without the consent of the two people most immediately concerned, for "reasons of State". No such reasons lie behind Princess Elizabeth's choice of a husband. If there is one thing more certain than any other about this Royal match, it is that the Princess was allowed unfettered freedom to make her choice, without suggestions or prompting from the King or any of his Ministers. There is one reason and one reason only for the marriage of Elizabeth and Philip, and it is the best reason of all: they are in love.

H.R.H. Prince Philip:
a study taken before he relinquished his Greek titles

CHAPTER TWO

Philip the Fair

SINCE Princess Elizabeth was looked on, and rightly looked on, as the most eligible girl in the world, the amount of public interest in her was exceeded only, in the five years between her first emergence into public life at sixteen and her twenty-first birthday, by the focus of world curiosity about the man whom she would marry. And that curiosity, legitimate enough in view of the high and responsible part the consort of the Heiress to the Throne may at any time be called upon to shoulder, is still, to a very large extent, unsatisfied even to-day, when the name of Philip Mountbatten has been blazoned from one end of the earth to the other, when his smiling face with its strong mouth and determined chin are familiar to everyone from newspaper pictures and news reels. For Lieutenant Mountbatten shares with our own Royal Family, among many other qualities, that of disliking publicity about his private life and affairs, and until the day when his name appeared first in the Court Circular, on the night of Wednesday, July 9, 1947, he regarded himself as a private citizen, his business as concerning none but himself.

For this reason, there are few pictures current of the former Prince before he became affianced to his Princess: and few stories are known about him in his early days.

To-day he is proud of two things, of his war-won British nationality (for his naturalisation as a British subject on February 26, 1947, was in no way the result of Court influence or priority demands by the King, but was his due as a foreign national who had served throughout the war in the British forces) and of his service and rank in the Royal Navy. Indeed, one of the best ways of assessing the character and personality of the man who has won the heart and affections of Princess Elizabeth is to visualise the traditional officer of the Royal Navy, silent about his job, modest about his attainments, ready and competent to deal with any situation, however difficult and unexpected, whose popularity among his men is all the more valuable because it is so entirely unsought.

Philip Mountbatten has all these attributes, and many more. Never seeking popularity in any way, he has been a most popular figure with his equals, superiors and inferiors, wherever he has been: at his Scottish public school with the other boys and his masters, at Dartmouth with cadets and instructors alike, as "Jimmy the One", or First Lieutenant, of two destroyers in wartime, equally on the lower-deck and in the wardroom. This quality of gaining popular esteem and affection without striving, so valuable and indeed necessary to members of the Royal House in a constitutional monarchy, was most clearly shown during the Scottish visit which followed almost immediately after the announcement of his engagement to Princess Elizabeth. In many quarters, as the pre-engagement rumours grew in strength, there had been a certain amount of ill-based feeling expressed against the match because of Philip's foreign blood. In Scotland, where for many a long year there had been hopes that the daughter of a queen of Scottish descent might find her own happiness with a Scotsman, this feeling was not altogether unknown. So when Philip came for the first time to Edinburgh as the betrothed of Princess Elizabeth there was appraisal in the Scottish eyes that were turned on him as he stepped from the Royal train at Princes Street Station.

But the Scots, shrewd judges, soon took him to their hearts, and Lord Provost Sir John Falconer spoke for all who had seen or met him when he said of Lieutenant Mountbatten at the Civic Lunch following the Princess's admission as a Free Burgess of Edinburgh, that his early years in Scotland and the fact that the destroyer in which he served three years during the war was named H.M.S. *Wallace*, gave him almost a claim to be regarded as a Scot: than which no higher compliment can fall from Scottish lips.

No one meeting Mountbatten and talking to him would take him for any but an Englishman. The only outward sign of his mixed blood is perhaps in his extreme fairness, for his hair is so blond, with reddish tints in the sunlight to give it almost the colour of new minted gold, that in the days of his Danish Viking ancestors he would undoubtedly have been known as Philip the Fair. He speaks English without the slightest trace of accent. It is to him his natural mother tongue, not only because it is in fact the language of his mother, Princess Alice, but because it was the first language he learned as a baby, and the language of his schooldays. More than mere language, it is the general attitude of a man to life that most defines his nationality: and nowhere is there a man with a more British outlook than Philip Mountbatten. The sea is in his blood, the Navy is his chosen career, and his most admired mentor is a man who, though himself not of pure English blood, has devoted his whole life and energies to Britain, and has won by his deeds in war and peace fresh lustre for the name of England, Rear Admiral the Viscount Mountbatten of Burma, whom Philip knows simply as "Uncle Dickie". "Uncle Dickie" has been the greatest single formative influence in moulding and building the character of his nephew, who, though the one is as dark as the other is fair, bears some small but distinct physical resemblance to him. No one who has had personal contact with or who has served under that brilliant leader of men can doubt what advantage it must be to a boy and a young man to have him as uncle, beau-ideal, and example.

And Lord Mountbatten, who, of course, was perfectly well aware of the ripening affection between his nephew and his young Royal cousin long before he left London to become last Viceroy of India, can, and almost certainly does, look with great and justified pride on the young man whom he has brought up almost as a son. Though it was not until 1944, when Philip was already twenty-four, that his father, Prince Andrew of Greece and Denmark, died at the age of sixty-two, ever since he was quite a small boy Philip's upbringing was to a large extent in the hands of his uncle. Prince Andrew, who had seen much of the political turmoil of Greece from the inside as a member of the reigning house and a general in the Greek Army, made up his mind early that his son should have the advantages of an education among his mother's people, and it was to an English preparatory school at Cheam, in Surrey, that the young Prince went for his first lessons. From there, he went to a school at Salem in Baden, Germany, where he would, it was planned, stay a year before returning to England to join a public school. It was a school run by a tall German of advanced views, who was already at deep variance with the Nazi regime, a quarrel that soon became open and resulted in the educationalist being banished from Hitler's Reich. But Mr. Kurt Hahn transferred his school and his views to a

The schoolboy Prince prepares for a high jump

About to play for Gordonstoun School : he is a keen cricketer

more congenial atmosphere, and set up a small public school at Gordonstoun, near the Scottish fishing village of Hopeman in Morayshire, perched high on the cliffs overlooking the North Sea, and there Philip followed him. Even had Mr. Hahn remained in Germany, however, his princely pupil would have left his Salem school, for to the well-balanced mind of the youngster of twelve years, there was something irresistibly comic about the Nazi salute with which his fellow pupils and their seniors greeted each other. Despite several warnings, Philip refused to conceal his mirth, and since this attitude was not exactly likely to endear him or his family—one of his sisters had married the son of Prince Max of Baden—to the authorities, it was decided to withdraw him at once.

Mr. Hahn, naturalised an Englishman, had the support of such well-known figures as the late Lord Tweedsmuir, Mr. Claude Elliott, Headmaster of Eton, and Admiral Sir Herbert Richmond for his new school, at which one hundred and seventy-eight boys, all of them from families of good standing, were enrolled. Among this small community, Prince Philip soon became popular, and soon found himself enjoying his new life very much. Mathematics and geography, both vital subjects for a future naval officer, were his favourite studies, and like most boys, it was at the subjects he liked best that he showed most promise. Besides normal athletics, the rare sport of javelin throwing was one of the exercises encouraged at this far from conventional school, and the boy whose ancestry was in Denmark, the home of javelin-throwing Vikings, showed, probably by mere coincidence, a natural aptitude for this, besides being an excellent runner and no mean performer at the high jump. In his last two years he developed into an all-round athlete, captaining the school at hockey and cricket, and finishing as head of the school, a position in which he first showed those qualities of leadership and sense of responsibility which stood him in such good stead later on in the Navy.

One experience he had as a schoolboy of fourteen and a half has been shared by few officers in the Royal Navy. For a day, he acted as assistant coastguard at Burghead.

At Gordonstoun, Philip was regarded with great favour both by Mr. Hahn and by the other masters. A certain bond of sympathy had already been set up between the banished schoolmaster and his pupil by their joint, though differently expressed, attitude to Hitler, and the older man's regard for his pupil was increased steadily as Philip began to show those virtues and qualities that are his to-day. He was keen,

Prince Philip goes to bat: he was captain of school cricket

At school he took a very great interest in amateur dramatics: Prince Philip (on left) took a minor part in " Macbeth"

intelligent and willing to learn, except for some subjects, Greek among them, which he privately thought were of little value to him. For he had already made up his mind about his future career. His family on his mother's side had a naval tradition established by his grandfather, the first Marquis of Milford Haven, who, as Prince Louis of Battenberg, was for so long First Sea Lord, and who did so much to ensure Britain's readiness for the naval war of 1914–18. That tradition was being carried forward with typical energy and enthusiasm by his uncle, then Lord Louis Mountbatten, and young Philip determined to follow in their footsteps if he could. But even in those early days he was showing signs of that sturdy independence of character that is one of his great charms. Hearing of his naval aspirations, a certain Very Important Person, on a visit to Gordonstoun, offered to do what he could to help him to enter the Service by dropping a word in the ears of influential folk at the Admiralty. But the young Prince refused the offer politely. "I'll get into the Navy on my own or not at all," said he, and that has been his way ever since.

For a boy with naval aspirations, Gordonstoun had many advantages. The fisherfolk of Hopeman knew the schoolboys well, for it is part of Mr. Hahn's educational theory to encourage his pupils to take part in village life, and young Prince Philip spent many happy hours out of the schoolroom, helping to scrape the bottoms of fishing boats, varnishing spars and going for sails. He was an enthusiastic member of

Lieutenant Mountbatten takes a class: Petty Officers listen to a lecture on current affairs

the school's Seamanship Guild, learning the difficult art of controlling a cutter under sail or oars, and taking part in two ambitious deep sea expeditions, one to the Norwegian coast and the other a cruise off the west coast of Scotland.

There is no surer testing ground for character than a small boat on a sea cruise, and Philip proved his worth to such an extent that his tutor, Commander John Lewty, reported that he was "a very cheerful shipmate, very conscientious in the carrying out of both major and minor duties, thoroughly trustworthy and not afraid of dirty and arduous work".

But he was, and still is, a person who enjoys fun, and who does not believe that all life is to be taken with grim seriousness. Whatever escapades were on, Philip would be in with the other boys, were it tantalising a village shopkeeper by making squeaking noises with wet fingers on a plate-glass window, or playing truant to have an unofficial swim. He was, by deliberate family orders, treated just like the other boys, an arrangement that suited him very well, for he did not like the fuss some people tried to make of him because of his Royal rank. Once, it is recorded, tired of being asked for his autograph by complete strangers, he obligingly took away a book and signed it—"Baldwin of Bewdley". After schooldays, this dislike of overmuch Royal fuss remained with him up to the day when he dropped his Royal rank and titles on naturalisation, but to people who approached him the right way, he would respond immediately, and the most treasured possession of a waitress in a certain well-known hotel to-day is the signature Prince Philip readily put in her autograph book when,

24

against the strict rules of the management, she asked him for it as she waited at table on him and a group of brother officers.

When the time came for him to enter the Royal Naval College at Dartmouth, his school report contained these sentences: "He is a born leader but he will need the exacting demands of a great service to do justice to himself. His best is outstanding." And Mr. Hahn, who forwarded that report, added privately that he regarded Philip as his best pupil, an opinion that was amply confirmed at Dartmouth where Philip was awarded both the King's Dirk as the best cadet of his term, and the Eardley-Howard-Crocket Prize as the best all-round cadet of the year. Both these early achievements showed that the young naval aspirant had already taken to heart the sage advice of his uncle to do everything with a will and to set out with the intention of winning. To win the King's Dirk, indeed, was for Philip something of a special achievement, for he was what is known at Dartmouth as a "Pub", that is a Special Entry Cadet, who has already received his preliminary education at a public school, as opposed to a "Dart" or a boy who entered the Royal Naval College direct from preparatory school, and the "Darts" have the advantage of a longer experience of naval ways. His career in the Navy after he left Dartmouth in 1940 bore out his early promise. As a sub-lieutenant, still pursuing his course of training, though he had already spent some time at sea in enemy waters, he gained four "firsts" and one "second" which gained him nine months' seniority out of a possible ten. Later still, as a full lieutenant, aged twenty-one and four months, he was appointed first lieutenant of the destroyer H.M.S. *Wallace*, the youngest officer in the Fleet to hold the post of executive officer in a ship of that size.

At the Methuen Arms: Lieutenant Mountbatten in the skittle alley

His first ship was the battleship *Ramillies*, which he joined as a midshipman with the Mediterranean Fleet, transferring to the cruiser *Kent* when *Ramillies* left the Med., and later to the *Shropshire*. In January, 1941, still a "snottie", he joined H.M.S. *Valiant*, and was one of the most popular members of the battleship's gunroom. What the other "snotties" particularly liked about their Royal messmate was his complete lack of "side" and his total disregard for his own Royal rank. Only once, according to his fellow midshipmen of those days, did he venture to use his rank for personal advantage. Rejoining his ship, he arrived aboard some three days after his fellows, and when an explanation was demanded by his senior officers, he blandly recounted that he had been detained in London owing to an urgent call to the Greek Embassy on business connected with the Greek Royal Family. Whether this explanation was accepted is not recorded, but the incident had no effect on the Prince's promotion.

He was gazetted sub-lieutenant on February 13th, 1942, and served aboard H.M.S. *Wallace*, a seventeen-year-old flotilla leader on the East Coast patrol, in that rank until he was promoted lieutenant in July, 1942, and posted as her second lieutenant.

But it was as a midshipman that Prince Philip fought his first and only major fleet action, at the Battle of Matapan. As midshipman in charge of a section of the searchlight control, he had one of the vital jobs in that swift deadly night action, when in the space of five minutes the British battleships *Valiant*, *Warspite* and *Barham* blew the Italian cruisers *Zara* and *Fiume* out of the water. For his coolness and efficiency as he held the enemy targets illuminated with *Valiant's* searchlights, he was mentioned in despatches by the C.-in-C., Admiral Sir Andrew (later Viscount) Cunningham. And, when the action was over, this was Prince Philip's description of the battle: "It was as near murder as anything could be in wartime. We just smashed the Italian cruisers. They burst into tremendous sheets of flame. I just hate to think how much worse it would have been for the Italian warships if we had met them by day instead of in a night action." Short as was that experience in time, it is not in minutes and hours that the depths of an experience can be assessed, and the Prince who sat drinking cocoa after the action, outwardly calm enough, inwardly as excited and elated as anyone on board, was a different, an older, and a wiser man than the Prince of half an hour earlier, before his ordeal by fire. Three months before, he had taken a few days leave, telling friends in London, "This is a dull war. There's no shooting."

After two years in the *Wallace*, during which he covered the Canadian landings in Sicily in her, he was given a new appointment, that of First Lieutenant of

Lieutenant Mountbatten inspecting divisions "aboard" H.M.S. King Arthur, *H.M. training establishment at Corsham*

H.M.S. *Whelp*, one of our latest destroyers, which was completed early in 1944. It was the kind of post coveted by all young lieutenants of the executive branch, and it went to Philip purely on his record for efficiency as officer responsible for discipline and internal organisation in the *Wallace*. A First Lieutenant can, from the ratings' point of view, make or mar a ship, and *Wallace* and *Whelp* were both among the happiest of ships, as anyone who served aboard either will agree. That state of affairs, so desirable in a captain's eyes, so important to the fighting efficiency of a warship, was in no small measure directly attributable to Lieutenant Prince Philip. It was partly this that his commanding officer had in mind when he described Prince Philip as the best second-in-command he had ever had.

Aboard H.M.S. *Whelp*, Prince Philip went East, with the British Pacific Fleet, under Admiral Lord Fraser: and his Supreme Commander was his always-admired Uncle Dickie—Admiral Mountbatten, then Allied Supreme Commander in South East Asia. But the hazards of war which threw the uncle and nephew together ruled that there should be no chance of Admiral Mountbatten mentioning his nephew in despatches, something that would have given him the very greatest pleasure, for the Japanese surrender followed quickly without any repetition of Matapan, and it was at the surrender of the Japanese Fleet in Tokyo Bay on September 2nd, 1945, that the two met for the first time for some years. It is fitting that this young man, destined to take his place in the history of the British Commonwealth, should have been present then, to see so dramatic a page of history in the writing.

Two other stories of Prince Philip's young days in the Navy are worth recording for the light they shed on his character. When he found himself at Melbourne in June, 1941, he was, like all other naval officers and ratings, made much of by the generous, open-hearted Australians. But Philip's personality has a way of impressing itself on all who meet him, and it was five years after this, when his name was already associated with that of Princess Elizabeth, that the crew of an aircraft bound from Australia to Britain noticed a twenty-five-pound fruit cake among the freight was addressed to "Lieutenant H.R.H. Prince Philip of Greece". His Melbourne friends had not forgotten him. The other story also comes from the Empire. Two R.N. midshipmen, off an armed merchant cruiser, had difficulty in manipulating their spoons and forks when they were being entertained ashore at Halifax, Nova Scotia. They explained their blisters were due to an unaccustomed spell as volunteer stokers, when the Chinese stokers went on strike. One of them was Prince Philip.

Long before he had even met Princess Elizabeth, Prince Philip had determined, like his uncle, on a naval career. When his engagement was announced, it was stated on the highest authority, that he intended to continue in the Service. That, without doubt, is his own wish. But, as in the case of Viscount Mountbatten, who had to leave his post as Admiral Commanding the Second Cruiser Squadron in April, 1947, when duty called him to Delhi as Viceroy, duty may take him away from his beloved navy, and it is difficult to see how the twin responsibilities of husband of the Heiress Presumptive and those of an ordinary serving naval officer could be reconciled. In the normal course, Lieutenant Mountbatten, with his first-class record and outstanding ability, could expect promotion as Lieutenant Commander in about three years' time: and then a further eight years would elapse before he received the third ring of a commander, for naval promotion is, to a large extent, governed by length of service in the various ranks. If he were to stay in the Navy, there is little doubt that he would achieve flag-rank, for, like his grandfather and uncle, he is undoubtedly the stuff of which Admirals are made. But the Navy's loss may be the Empire's gain.

Princess Elizabeth's first autograph: she gave copies of this portrait, taken when she was seven, to Indian Princes who were guests of the Duke and Duchess of York at 145 Piccadilly.

CHAPTER THREE

Marriage and the Constitution

THE ROMANCE and marriage of any Princess are matters of wide and compelling interest, for marriage is one of the great experiences open to all mankind, whereas Princesses are creatures apart, retaining, no matter what their age or looks, a certain attraction bequeathed them by the idealised Princesses of our fairy tales. When the Princess in question is twenty-one and decidedly attractive in her own right, without any need to go borrowing from fairyland, the interest is all the greater: and when the Princess is also the heiress to a vast empire, the future wearer of the world's mightiest crown, the person on whom are set the affections and hopes of five great nations, each of which will one day claim her as Queen, the interest becomes world-wide, and embraces students of politics and diplomats as well as ordinary romance-loving folk.

Princess Elizabeth's marriage is unquestionably a national, or rather an empire, event of the utmost importance. Though her husband can never ascend the British Throne, or even share it with his wife, the position of consort to the future Queen is one of such far-reaching influence and potentiality that it is right for the constitutional aspects of the marriage to be examined.

Since 1772, when the Royal Marriages Act was passed, in the sixteenth year of George III, the matrimonial plans of any member of the reigning house in the line of succession to the British throne have been recognised as a matter of national concern. If a sovereign, or a potential sovereign, makes a bad marriage, it contains within itself the possibility, if not the probability, of a national disaster, a condition which, true enough two hundred years ago, is doubly true to-day when it is on the person of the sovereign and the example of his or her home life that the very cohesion of the scattered Units of the British Commonwealth—as the former Dominions are now officially and cumbersomely known—depends. Contrary to general belief, the Royal Marriages Act, whose terms explicitly govern the whole of Princess Elizabeth's marriage, as they did that of her father, do not give control of Royal matches into the hands of Parliament. The Princess had not to seek the consent of either House before she became engaged to Lieutenant Mountbatten, nor had the King to go either to his "faithful Commons" or to the House of Lords for sanction for the match. It is on the King himself that the Act of George III lays the responsibility of deciding whether or not a suitor is a fit and proper person to marry into the line of succession. It was therefore the King's consent which was necessary before the Princess's engagement, let alone her marriage, could legally take place.

"No descendant of His late Majesty George II, male or female (other than the issue of Princesses who have married or who may marry into foreign families), shall be capable of contracting matrimony without the previous consent of His Majesty, his heirs and successors, signified under the Great Seal," is the significant wording of the Act.

Actually, Princess Elizabeth's engagement was announced officially three weeks before the special meeting of the Privy Council at which the King made the declaration of his "consent to the contracting of matrimony". This is in accordance with long established custom whereby the Sovereign first gives his private consent as a parent,

Where she came of age: the Princess walks with her family in the colourful gardens of Government House, Cape Town

but announces it publicly in his Court Circular, and later gives his official and formal consent to the union "in Council".

Should the Sovereign refuse his consent, and the intending Royal bride or bridegroom being aged over twenty-five persist in marrying, the old Act provides a loophole, allowing the marriage to be solemnised provided twelve months' notice be given to the Privy Council—unless both Houses of Parliament declare their disapproval. No such question, of course, arose in the case of Princess Elizabeth and Philip.

Some misapprehension exists, particularly in the Dominions, about the reason for and the purpose of this pre-marriage Council. Strictly speaking, it is a legal, and not a constitutional, step, though the exact borderline between the law and the constitution is so vague and shadowy that not even the greatest experts can always agree on its precise definition. The King's declaration in Council is, in effect, the reading of banns for the marriage of a member of the Royal Family, and the fact that Princess Elizabeth happens to be heiress to the throne had little to do with the necessity for the holding of a Council before she could legally marry. The same procedure applies in the case of even the remotest descendants of George II, and there have been, within recent years, two or three cases of foreign princelings, descended from him, who have written to the King asking his consent to their marriages, though they were so far removed from the present Royal Family that the King had never met them. The Council which the King held at Buckingham Palace on Thursday, July 31, 1947, was not, therefore, for the purpose of giving assent to the intended marriage of the Heiress to the Throne, but to allow the King to declare—by reading aloud from a parchment scroll—his consent to the petition to marry put to him by one member of his House, in this case his elder daughter.

The presence of the four Empire representatives, Mr. C. D. Howe, Minister of Reconstruction and Supply in the Canadian Government, Mr. J. A. Beasley, High Commissioner for Australia, Mr. W. J. Jordan, High Commissioner for New Zealand, and Mr. J. Stratford, former Chief Justice of the Union of South Africa, was not constitutionally necessary, for the ordinary quorum of four members of the Privy Council would have sufficed. But King George V, with one of those happy inspirations of monarchy which were part of his strength, called Empire representatives to the Privy Council at which he consented to the marriage of the late Duke of Kent, the first Royal marriage to follow the passing of the Statute of Westminster, remarking that it would be much better and more fitting to make the marriage Council an "Empire family party". Since then, that precedent has been followed.

Princess Elizabeth was not present at the Privy Council meeting which determined her future: nor had she the right to be, for up to now, she has not been "admitted"—members of the Royal Family are not sworn in like other Counsellors—to her father's Council.

After the Council, two more steps were necessary before the constitutional and legal formalities were complete, the affixing of the Great Seal to the instrument setting forth the King's consent to "the contracting of matrimony between her Royal Highness Elizabeth Alexandra Mary and Lieutenant Philip Mountbatten, R.N., son of the late Prince Andrew of Greece and Princess Andrew (Princess Alice of Battenberg);" and the preparation by the Archbishop of Canterbury, on a warrant from the King, of the special licence for a Royal marriage.

Another and equally important Act controlling all marriages within the British Royal Family is the "Bill of Rights", passed in the first year of the reign of William and Mary, when England was still settling down after the religious troubles that were a legacy of the Revolution. The act for Declaring the Rights and Liberties of the Subject, and Settling the Succession of the Crown (1 W & M, C2.) expressly bars succession to the Crown from all persons holding communion with the Church of Rome, or marrying "a Papist". Should any member of the Royal House persist in an alliance with such a person, the Act rules that the people are absolved of their allegiance and the Crown descends "to such person or persons being Protestant as should have inherited and enjoyed the same, in case the said person or persons so reconciled, holding communion or professing (the Church of Rome) or marrying, as aforesaid, were naturally dead".

Princess Elizabeth watches native girl guides in Rhodesia

A great moment. H.M.S. Vanguard *with the Royal Family aboard enters Duncan Dock, Cape Town*

Members of the Greek Orthodox Church, in which Lieutenant Mountbatten was baptised, do not, of course, fall within the category of those defined by the Act as disturbing the natural order of succession, for the Greek Orthodox Church is in full communion with the Established Church of England, and Lieutenant Mountbatten has been a regular attendant at Church of England worship throughout his career in the Navy.

Apart from these restrictions, Princess Elizabeth was as free as any other girl to make her choice of a husband. But the marriage of the Heiress Presumptive must of necessity be a matter of much more than mere family interest, and the King, though bound by no constitutional edict to do so, acquainted in advance all his Prime Ministers in the Commonwealth, Mr. Mackenzie King of Canada, Mr. Chifley of Australia, Mr. Fraser of New Zealand, Field-Marshal Smuts of South Africa, and Mr. de Valera in Eire, as well as Mr. Attlee, with his intention to consent to the proposed betrothal. The Premiers of Southern Rhodesia and of Northern Ireland were informed later through the U.K. government. Because the development of the Commonwealth is so much a matter of gradual natural change and evolution so little defined by statute, there are no precise rules clarifying this position.

But the highest authorities take the view that, following the precedent set at the time of the Abdication, each of His Majesty's Prime Ministers has the right to express, on behalf of the Government of which he is the head, disapprobation, and to offer comments, though the consent of none of these Governments, as stated above, is constitutionally necessary.

In the present case, each and every one of the Governments to whom the King conveyed his intentions, at once expressed their full approval and tendered their congratulations. It is possible to think that no warmer or more heartfelt congratulations can have come than those from "General" Smuts, the veteran thinker and statesman of Empire, who, so short a time before, had watched with pride and pleasure the Princess growing to full womanhood and widening her own horizon, as she journeyed triumphantly across the spacious veldt and through the thriving cities and towns of his beloved South Africa.

Princess Elizabeth's personal position, from the constitutional aspect, cannot be changed or affected by her altered status as a married woman. She remains, and always will remain, during the lifetime of the King, Heiress Presumptive to the Crown. The fact that Lieutenant Mountbatten marries the King's elder daughter had no effect at all on the line of succession to the Throne. Princess Margaret remains second in succession, the Duke of Gloucester third, then his children, then the young Duke of Kent, his brother and sister, then the Earl of Harewood (as elder son of the Princess Royal) and his brother, the Hon. Gerald Lascelles. Children of Princess Elizabeth would, of course, come immediately after her in the succession. A son, whether the first born or not, would become second in succession, followed by daughters according to their age, with Princess Margaret and the others named above following in that order.

Should Princess Elizabeth come to the throne, she would reign as full Queen Regnant, just as would be the case if she were unmarried. Her husband would be the Sovereign's Consort, but would not have any claim to the title of King. Nor need he be necessarily given the title of Prince Consort, which Queen Victoria, with the approval of Parliament, bestowed on her husband, Prince Albert, only after seventeen years of life together, during all of which time she was Queen. The predominance of the wife, from the constitutional point of view, as the Royal partner in the union is emphasised by the fact that marriage does not change Princess Elizabeth's surname. She remains a Princess of the Royal House of Windsor, and retains, too, her own coat of arms, the Royal Arms of England, differenced by her cadency label of three points in argent, the centre point charged with the Tudor Rose, each of the other two with the Cross of St. George. These will be her arms until she becomes Queen, when the "cadency label" disappears and she assumes the Royal Arms, as Sovereign and Head of the House of Windsor. In the case of a Prince of the Blood marrying, his wife quarters the Royal Arms with those of her own family, as did Her Majesty the Queen, whose personal standard, always to be seen flying over Buckingham Palace when she is in residence alone, bears the Royal Arms quartered with the black bows and the azure lion rampant of the Bowes-Lyon family.

The position of the consort to a Queen in the British monarchy may be summarised by saying that he shares her life but not her throne. Queen Victoria, throughout her married life, was at pains to separate her family relations with her beloved husband from the constitutional relations of a sovereign and her subject. Thus, she insisted on the inclusion of the word "obey" in her marriage service, though there seemed, to some of her advisers, something incongruous in the reigning Queen promising to obey anyone else. But Queen Victoria, with that sagacity that made her so strong a Queen, explained that she would obey as a wife, but rule as a Queen.

Since the days of Albert the Good, there have been many changes in the duties and powers of the occupant of the throne, changes which must also affect the consort of its occupant. Albert, with his immense devotion to work, his eager, inquiring mind, and his capacity for absorbing information, made himself an indispensable assistant to Victoria in carrying out many of her queenly duties. He was, in effect, an extraordinarily efficient and painstaking private secretary to the Queen, as well as a devoted and loving husband. Reviewing the duties of his own position, he wrote words of guidance to consorts who might follow after him, which may be quoted again here: "The husband (of a female Sovereign) should entirely sink his own *individual* existence in that of his wife. He should aim at no power by himself, or for himself, should shun all contention, assume no separate responsibility before the public but make his position entirely a part of hers . . . be able to assist and advise her at any moment in any of the multifarious and difficult questions or duties brought before her, sometimes international, sometimes political, social or personal." To-day, the office of Private Secretary to the Sovereign has developed so greatly in importance, and embraces so wide a range of duties, since the Private Secretary is now equally concerned with the business that passes between the King and each of his separate Governments in the Commonwealth, that it is difficult to imagine a similar situation to that of Queen Victoria's day arising now. But, even with the purely secretarial side removed, much of what Prince Albert wrote, with his own personal experience to give strength to his words, holds good to-day. Another appreciation of the duties of the Prince Consort, also from one in an excellent position to observe, since she was his daughter, occurs in the Memoirs of Princess Alice, Grand Duchess of Hesse, who was Queen Victoria's second daughter, and, by a turn of fate, great-grandmother of Lieutenant Mountbatten. "By his strength of character, and rare energy of intellect, combined with a thorough self-control, and an unswerving devotion to the duties of his position, he succeeded in gaining the love and esteem of a nation

When Queen Victoria married : at the Chapel Royal, St. James's, February 10, 1840

which, though it keeps watch over its rights and privileges with peculiar jealousy, knows also how to show great generosity, when once it has learned to love and to trust. . . . In his position of intimate confidential adviser to the Sovereign, he showed the greatest tact, and gained the affection and respect of the Ministers who succeeded one another at the head of affairs, whilst the more he became known the more his genuine worth was appreciated by the nation at large," wrote the Royal lady whose great-grandson was destined to wed the Heiress to Queen Victoria's fourth successor on the throne; proving that Albert had fulfilled the conditions predicated by wise King Leopold of the Belgians, that "if he does not at the outset accept it as a vocation of grave responsibility there is small likelihood of his succeeding."

Comparisons between the Prince Consort and the husband of Princess Elizabeth seem easy to make, but actually the positions of the two are very different. When Albert came to England in 1839, it was the Queen, the reigning Sovereign, to whom he became betrothed and later married. Lieutenant Mountbatten became engaged to the heiress to the throne, and, from the viewpoint of the lawyer and the constitutionalist, there is a world of difference between the two, for it is not difficult to conceive of circumstances in which the Heiress Presumptive to a throne might never in fact become its occupant. For this reason such matters as the granting of new titles and dignity to the former Prince of Greece and Denmark were matters on which the King had to make decisions unguided by precedents, for there were no exact precedents to follow. To find a parallel case of the Sovereign's daughter who is also his heiress marrying, we must go back eight centuries to Princess Maud, daughter of King Henry I, who married in 1127. In this connection, it is interesting to note that the style of Royal Highness and the title of Prince Consort were bestowed on Albert, who

Her parents' wedding: at Westminster Abbey on April 26, 1923

was already a Highness in his own right, by Act of Parliament, passed at the instigation of the Queen. She took this course, presumably, because of the important issues involved in the granting of a new title to one so close to the Throne: for it is quite within the power of the Sovereign to bestow the rank of Royal Highness at his own discretion by Letters Patent under the Great Seal, as was done by his present Majesty in the case of the Duke of Windsor, who had relinquished all his Royal style and titles at his abdication.

However different the cases may be from the purist's standpoint, everyone today seeing Princess Elizabeth in her new-found happiness, and looking at the man who has brought it to her, must recall the man who brought that same happiness to Queen Victoria: and there can be no doubt that Philip's vocation, like Albert's, is one of grave responsibility. Nor can there be any doubt, from the qualities he has already shown in his career as a fighting officer of the Royal Navy, that Philip is a man who can accept responsibility with a firm confidence. When, on the evening of the official engagement day, Philip stepped for the first time onto the red-hung balcony of Buckingham Palace, to hear the crowds cheer him and his Princess, as they stood side by side with the King and Queen, he was stepping into a new life. He stepped not merely from the softly-lit comfort of the Palace room out onto the balcony, but also from the quiet privacy of life as a naval officer, with its limited responsibilities and wide opportunities, into the glare and limelight of a life in which privacy is so rare and hard to win that it becomes the most treasured possession of all, a life whose path is clearly and strictly set out, and whose opportunities are circumscribed by the rules and conventions of Royal usage. But he, whose family history had taught him something of the darker possibilities of Royal life (his grandfather George I of Greece was assassinated) stepped across the chasm dividing private from public life with the easy bearing and the smile of a man who knows his own mind and has proved himself no weakling.

The engagement smile:
a picture taken at Buckingham Palace
on the day of the announcement

CHAPTER FOUR

Engagement Days

OUTSIDE Brodick Castle, the lovely home of the Duke and Duchess of Montrose in the holiday Isle of Arran off the Ayrshire coast, a line of gleaming big cars waited. It was a great day in Arran history, the first Royal visit to the Isle since Edward VII and Queen Alexandra paid a surprise visit in 1902, explaining to the then Duke and Duchess, who had hurried down from the shooting lodge at Dougrie to greet them, that from the Royal yacht the island looked so beautiful that they could not pass it without landing. At the other side of the Castle, the tall, kilted Duke of Montrose and his kindly, charming Duchess, were pointing out views and showing the Castle gardens to the King and Queen, Princess Elizabeth, Princess Margaret, and Lieutenant Philip Mountbatten. The little party turned to walk to the cars, and Lieutenant Mountbatten spoke to the King, who smiled, and remarked "It's a very heavy car". Chauffeurs and detectives stood by the waiting cars; the King and Queen entered the first with Princess Margaret and the Duke and Duchess. Then Mountbatten opened the *front* door of the second car, a big black limousine from the Royal Mews, helped his fiancée in, and took his seat beside her at the driving wheel, while an astonished chauffeur and an equally surprised detective sat in unusual luxury and state in the rear, as the Royal procession moved off for a two hours' drive round the island. The island roads have sharp turns and bends, with occasionally alarming glimpses of the sea far beneath, but Mountbatten handled the car, which weighs over a ton and a half, with confident ease, taking a hand off the wheel now and then to wave back at the cheering, delighted crowds, while Princess Elizabeth happily enjoyed this new experience. Perhaps the chauffeur in the back, thinking of the small sports car which Lieutenant Mountbatten usually drives, and the different technique of cornering in the big car on an unfamiliar road, did not enjoy the first few minutes quite so much.

That small incident tells a great deal about the character and personality of the man of Princess Elizabeth's choice. He is not one to be easily put off by empty convention, or to be deterred from a course of action because of lack of precedent. His strong chin, firm mouth, and steady blue eyes do not belie him. As you might expect of a naval officer, he does not allow himself to be dominated by circumstances, but takes easy charge of a situation, with a smiling charm that makes people eager to do what he wishes. He has much the same forceful, dynamic personality as his uncle, Lord Mountbatten, though it is veiled most of the time, as was Lord Louis' at the same age, by a disarming, easy-going friendliness. These qualities that made him a leader, and a most popular leader, at school at Gordonstoun, among the "pubs" or Special Entry boys at Dartmouth, in the gunroom as a midshipman, and later as a responsible destroyer officer, are the very qualities most needed for the difficult, responsible role that will be his in the future. Strong-willed and decided once his mind is made up, he has a calm judgment that stops him from impetuosity. Another

Philip takes the wheel; a royal drive without precedent

of his marked qualities, and again one of the utmost value in the crowded, sometimes repetitive life of constitutional royalty, is that of being interested in all he sees. To a Land Girl tending cattle, he will talk about butter-fat content, and other farming mysteries, to a cameraman filming the Royal party he will talk about lenses and exposures, and to a local councillor he will talk of housing problems. Nor is he a man to be fobbed off with half answers. He has, again like his uncle, the gift of easily assimilating and long retaining knowledge on all manner of topics. A public pointer to this side of his character can be seen in his recent visits to the House of Commons. A naval officer gets but little opportunity for studying the workings of the British system of Government, save by reading books, and in the future it is obviously going to be of great importance for him to know a good deal about the way our Government functions under a constitutional monarchy. Whatever is necessary to know for any job he is called on to do, he will learn. That has always been his rule of life, and he is likely in future to be a familiar figure in the Distinguished Strangers Gallery or in the new special gallery to be built for Princess Elizabeth in the new House of Commons.

To be constantly exposed to public attention, to have hundreds of eyes turned on your every movement, to be filmed and photographed wherever you go, these are part of the everyday ritual of modern royalty. Even to those accustomed to it from birth, it must remain something of an ordeal, and to one suddenly put into the very centre of the limelight the ordeal is correspondingly greater. So the seven days he spent in Scotland after the engagement announcement, appearing for the first time as a member of the Royal party, were in the nature of a trial—and no easy trial—run

The Princess photographed with her future fiancé at the marriage of her lady-in-waiting, the Honourable Mrs. Vicary Gibbs, to the Honourable Andrew Elphinstone, the Princess's cousin, on May 29th, 1946

The Royal pair go off for a walk in the grounds of Buckingham Palace

for Lieutenant Philip. He emerged from it with flying colours and a greatly enhanced popularity. "If he goes on like this, he'll become one of the most popular men in the country," said one shrewd observer, not given to easy praise, after spending the week following the Royal party.

What the cameramen think of public figures is often an accurate, though rarely made public, guide to their worth. The men with the Press cameras are used to seeing great figures on the world's stage in all sorts of circumstances, and their opinions are not without value. Nearly every photographer in Britain will agree, for example, that Her Majesty the Queen is the best of all "subjects", a view which in different words expressed the world's opinion of the Queen. After a week with Lieutenant Mountbatten, they marked him down as a friend, and that is high praise. For his part, Lieutenant Mountbatten derives—as does Princess Elizabeth—a certain mild amusement from watching the antics of some of the cameramen who contort themselves into extraordinary postures in attempts to get some different "angle" for their pictures. After watching an exhibition of this kind one day with the Princess, the Lieutenant surprised one photographer afterwards by going over and congratulating him. "Thank you, sir, but what for?" asked the recipient of the congratulations. "Because you are the only one who stands up straight and takes the photograph without a lot of contortions. We've been watching you," said Mountbatten.

Mountbatten had been under "ordeal by (camera) fire" before. In the days when his name was first linked with that of Princess Elizabeth, photographers, under instructions from their offices, chased him a good deal, but with scant success, for he did his best to elude them. Now with the photographers present officially, he gave them every chance. It was on the morning of the engagement announcement that he had his first official pictures taken with Princess Elizabeth, in the Bow Room at Buckingham Palace, that pleasant red-carpeted room with its long french windows opening on to the gardens in the semi-circle that gives the room its name. This is perhaps the most familiar of all the rooms at Buckingham Palace to the outside public, for it is through this apartment that the bulk of guests at the Royal garden parties pass on their way to the spacious lawns. Inside the room and out on the Palace terrace, the young couple sat and walked while one photographer and one newsreel man took their pictures for all the world to see. Neither the Princess nor her fiancé were made-up for the occasion, and as any film expert will tell you, to have yourself "shot" by a cine-camera without make-up is by no means the way to ensure that you will look your best on the screen: and the resultant film of the betrothed couple certainly did not flatter Mountbatten's looks.

So far, his voice has not been heard on the radio. When it is, the public will hear a deep, firm, pleasant voice, with a decided touch of authority in it, and no trace whatever of any foreign accent. There is, indeed, no reason at all why Mountbatten should have any accent, since English has been his natural tongue since his earliest years. He is a good impromptu speaker, with little nervousness in his manner. Just a few days before the engagement announcement, he went to the tercentenary celebrations of his old prep. school, Tabors, now moved from Cheam to Headley, in Berkshire. Called on to speak, he said, "I feel like a new boy again," but went on for some eight minutes without notes, striking just the right note when he said he was one of the generation whose parents had spent money on their education only for them to be "snapped up by the Services" during the past war. "We were just old enough to go out and be killed," said Mountbatten, who lost many of his own friends and schoolfellows in the war. "I am one of the lucky ones, but a lot will not be coming home again."

That was the only public speech he had made before the engagement. But he is

*Their first public appearance together: at the Palace
garden party which followed the engagement announcement*

a practised and fluent speaker, as scores of newly fledged petty officers in the post-war Royal Navy well know. At H.M.S. *King Arthur*, otherwise the "stone frigate" or shore-training establishment for petty officers at Corsham, Wiltshire, he spent the best part of a year as lecturer on leadership, sea warfare and current affairs—and to lecture a class of eager young P.O.s on current affairs demands a really thorough knowledge of what you are talking about, coupled with an ability to deal with questions expected and unexpected, and a strong sense of humour. Mountbatten has all three, and was one of the most popular and successful instructors at the school. Though he knew very well that a complete change in his life must come soon, and though many if not all of his students guessed they were sitting under the probably future Prince Consort of England, he never allowed that to affect his work at the training school in any way. He joined in all the school fun, took part in all games, including skittles, that ancient and skilful pastime of the English inns. As a member of the "ship's" team, he frequently played in the "alley" at the Methuen Arms in Corsham, where regular customers regarded him, in the words of one of them, as "a cheery and unassuming bloke, whom everyone likes". What better recommendation could there be?

Many months before the engagement, Lord Mountbatten, then in London, decided, with his far-sighted vision, that if, as seemed likely, his good-looking nephew and the Heiress of England were falling in love, it was time that Prince Philip was introduced to some of the people who would be chiefly concerned in making him known, as he would have to be known, to a wider public. So Lord Mountbatten, who had met and made friends with many Fleet Street editors during their Service days, invited several of them, together with a few M.P.s and other public men, to meet Philip informally over a glass of sherry, in the Mountbattens' hospitable home in Chester Street, S.W.1. What the editors saw, they liked. No one meeting Philip could help but like him, with his good looks, his manifest intelligence, his modest demeanour, his easy manners and his lively conversation. At this time, of course, the Princess and Philip were definitely not engaged, and Mountbatten explained to his friends, with complete candour, that he did not know, nor would he ask, if his young nephew and the King's daughter would

Lieutenant Mountbatten applauds as his fiancée receives the scroll of freedom after her speech in Edinburgh

or would not become betrothed. But it was an excellent move, for it enabled those who guide the policies of the great national newspapers to decide for themselves what kind of man this was, and to clear their minds of lurking prejudices against him because of his foreign birth and membership of the not over-popular Greek Royal Family, in a direct way that would not have been possible otherwise. When the engagement was at last announced, editors and others responsible for moulding public opinion had their own opinions, based on first-hand acquaintance with the Prince, to shape their views. And the general view of the editors and others was almost identical, though expressed in different words, with that of the "regulars" of the Methuen Arms.

Of all things that distinguish the British from other nations, first perhaps is their attitude to sport. It is an integral part of British life, yet the British do not, as some people do, allow sport to dominate their lives. In this, no one could be more British than Philip Mountbatten. After captaining his school at cricket and hockey, he had, in his days on a gunnery course at Whale Island, Portsmouth, otherwise H.M.S. *Vernon*, the Navy's gunnery school, the unusual honour of an invitation from the lower deck to play football for the "ship", a tribute both to his ability at football and to his popularity with the men, for officers are rarely asked to play in *Vernon's* soccer eleven. In his battleship days, he would seize any and every chance of a game of cricket, but he never let sport interfere with the more serious business of equipping himself for a naval career. It is a strange thing that this most popular of young men has never apparently had a nickname. At school he was known as Prince Philip or Philip, at Dartmouth as Cadet Philip, and later, aboard ship, his single name did dual work as a surname in orders and on official occasions, as a Christian name in the gunroom or wardroom mess.

For his war service, Philip earned five decorations, the Atlantic Star, the African Star, the Burma Star, with the Pacific rosette, the Italian Star and the Victory medal with the laurels of a "mention in despatches". He also has the Coronation Medal and three Greek medals, the Greek Military Cross, awarded him for his services at the Battle of Matapan, the Order of the Redeemer Second Class, and the Order of St. Constantine and St. George Fourth Class, with swords.

Meeting Philip Mountbatten for the first time, many people are struck by a likeness which they cannot quite place. He seems to remind them of someone, but of whom they are not quite sure. To those in any way connected with the Royal Family, the answer is easy. It is the late Duke of Kent whom Philip resembles, not so much in facial appearance, but in many other ways. The way he stands and walks, the way he holds his head, the easy elegance with which he wears his clothes, all are very reminiscent of the attractive young Duke who died so suddenly in a wartime air crash. And Mountbatten has many of the attractive attributes that made the Duke of Kent one of the most popular of the Royal Family. He is not only fond of dancing, but is an extremely good dancer. He dresses well with quiet taste. Like Kent, who used to run three miles a day in shorts and sweater to keep himself fit, he is a great believer in open air and exercise. One of his favourite forms of exercise is swimming, which he learned as a small boy on the Morayshire Coast, and which, as he was fond of instilling into the ears of all men under his command, is an almost invaluable accomplishment for a sailor. He is also extremely fond of driving fast sports cars, an art at which he is something of an expert. Not many months ago, he acquired a small British open two-seater renowned for its turn of speed, the kind of car in which the driver sits almost horizontally, and feels himself as much at one with his car as a good rider is at one with his horse. He does not ride, for sailors have but little chance in wartime to learn, but undoubtedly Princess Elizabeth, with her own great interest in horses, will persuade him to take up this other accomplishment to complete his enjoyment of the outdoor life he loves.

Neither a teetotaller nor a non-smoker, Philip likes to drink a glass of beer ashore, or a pink gin—favourite wardroom drink—afloat. He enjoys wine with meals, but does not set himself up as a connoisseur. He smokes cigarettes, and occasionally a cigar.

He dislikes ostentation in any shape or form and the only jewellery he permits himself is a heavy gold signet ring with his own family arms, the Greek cross on a plain shield, with the arms of Denmark in the centre. This ring he wears on his left-hand little finger. His handwriting is firm and clear, with a very slight backward slope.

Lieutenant Mountbatten takes his Princess to a ball in Edinburgh : it was their first appearance together at a charity dance

CHAPTER FIVE

Family Background

O N JUNE 10, 1921, in a pleasant house of moderate size, with the not very original name of Mon Repos, on the Island of Corfu, in the Mediterranean, His Royal Highness Prince Philip of Greece and Denmark was born, latest scion of one of the oldest Royal Houses in Europe. His father was Prince Andrew, a general in the Greek Army of his elder brother, King Constantine I. His mother was Princess Alice of Battenberg, named after her grandmother, Queen Victoria's second daughter, Alice. It is a peculiarity of the Greek Royal House to give only one Christian name to its children, instead of the four or six that are customary among most royal families, and the tradition was not broken for the young Prince, who received at his baptism into the Greek Orthodox Church the single name of Philip.

He had not borne it long, when the noise of revolution came to disturb the quietude of Mon Repos, and a detachment of British sailors, from the Navy in which later he was himself to serve, had to rescue the baby Prince and his parents from a wild mob which threatened them with death. His father, though a Prince of Greece, born in Athens itself, had no very strong connections with Greece, for the House of Schleswig-Holstein-Sonderburg-Glucksburg had come to the throne of Greece only fifty-eight years earlier, when the Greek National Assembly offered the throne to Prince William of Denmark, son of the famed King Christian the Ninth, whose daughter became Britain's Queen Alexandra. So he withdrew, with but little regret, from the stormy scene of Greek politics, to the seclusion of an estate at St. Cloud, near Paris, and there settled down to live happily in exile with his wife, their four daughters and their one son. As he surveyed the violent flux of events in Greece from the distance, Prince Andrew decided, with the very full support and approval of his wife, that the small Prince Philip should be brought up in England. Even in those early days, Princess Alice, whose father, the first Marquess of Milford Haven, had, as Prince Louis of Battenberg, been an Admiral of the Fleet and First Sea Lord at the British Admiralty, had hopes that her son would elect to follow his grandfather and make the Royal Navy his career. When he was quite small, he began to take his holidays with his grandmother, the Dowager Marchioness of Milford Haven, who, like most grandmothers, was devoted to the little boy. She followed his career with the closest interest, and when, lying on a sick bed at Kensington Palace at the age of eighty-four, she heard of his engagement, no one was more genuinely delighted. It was during these early holidays that young Lord Louis Mountbatten first began to take notice of his nephew, and it was then, too, at Kensington Palace, in the heavily-decorated Victorian rooms that were his grandmother's home, and at the Milford Haven country estate at Lynden Manor, near Maidenhead, that plans for his education in England were drawn up.

Already, Prince Philip had been to Buckingham Palace. It was as a baby-in-arms, at the age of three months, that he first drove through the tall iron gates of the Palace, when he came to England with his father and mother to attend the funeral of his grandfather, the Marquis of Milford Haven, who died in 1921 at the age of sixty-seven. Now, he began to spend less and less of his time in Paris, and more and more in London or Maidenhead, till the day came for him to go to his first real school (he had attended occasional classes at St. Cloud, where he acquired his first French and the groundwork of an accent that is excellent to-day). It was to "Tabor's" the well-known preparatory school at Cheam, established nearly three hundred years earlier, that the seven-year-old Prince went, on the advice of "Uncle Dickie". From then on, Philip's connection with his family grew somewhat tenuous. He saw his father and his sisters, now growing into very attractive young women, but infrequently; of his mother, who came often to see her mother, at Kensington, he saw more; and of his Greek relations, practically nothing. Indeed, up to his engagement at the age of twenty-six, Philip had spent altogether no more than fifteen months in the country of his birth, and never learned to speak or read modern Greek. Though there was no formal act of guardianship, Lord Louis, with the full consent of his brother-in-law and sister, took more and more charge of Philip's affairs. Without a son himself, Lord Louis lavished warm affection as well as sage advice on the boy, who, with this strong influence behind him, grew up as English in ways and outlook as though he had no foreign blood in him.

Actually, Philip Mountbatten has a mixture of British, Danish, Russian and German ancestry. His paternal grandfather was a Dane, Prince William, afterwards King George I of Greece. His paternal grandmother was a Russian, the Grand Duchess Olga of the House of Romanoff. On his mother's side, his grandparents were Princess Victoria of England, and Prince Louis of Battenberg, himself a naturalised British subject, and a firm believer in the British way of life. Of actual Greek blood, he has none. Before his engagement, he had another connection by marriage with the British Royal Family through his first cousin Princess Marina, the Duchess of Kent.

Princess Elizabeth and Philip have two ancestors in common, Queen Victoria, whose great-great-grandchildren they both are, and King Christian the Ninth of Denmark, great-great-grandfather to Princess Elizabeth, and great-grandfather to Philip.

His three sisters are married to Germans. The eldest, forty-two-year-old Princess Margarita, is wife of Prince Godfrey of Hohenlohe-Langenburg; Princess Theodora, aged forty-one, is married to the Margrave of Baden; and the youngest, thirty-three-year-old Princess Sophia, widow of Prince Christopher of Hesse, married the Prince of Hanover a year ago. But the sisters and their brother have seen very little of each other since long before the war days, and the marriage of Princess Sophia at Lake Constance last year was the first family reunion for many years. His fourth sister, Princess Cecilia, who was married to the Grand Duke of Hesse, was killed in an air crash in 1937.

The war, indeed, cut Prince Philip almost entirely off from his family. His father died in 1944, at the age of sixty-two. His mother, tall and stately Princess Alice, spent the whole of the war years in Athens, in company with her sister-in-law Princess Nicholas of Greece, the Duchess of Kent's mother. Both Princesses worked with the Swedish and Swiss Red Cross in Greek hospitals. Princess Alice came to this country in October, 1946, for a short stay, and returned in April, 1947, primarily, she said, to be with her mother, whose doctor had advised her that she was very ill. A further reason, and a happier one, was the prospect of the engagement announcement.

It was on February 28, 1947, that Prince Philip's long-cherished ambition of becoming a British subject was at last achieved. Because of the war, he had had to wait six years for the application he put in as a young midshipman to materialise, and, with rumours continuously linking his name with that of Princess Elizabeth, the public concluded, quite erroneously, that this naturalisation was an essential preliminary to his forthcoming engagement to the Heiress Presumptive. His decision to seek British nationality had in fact nothing to do with his matrimonial intentions, but when, in October, 1946, these intentions were crystallising, he asked, with the full approval of the King, that no extra priority should be given to his application because of what might be going to happen. This request, typical of the modest young Prince, was also a significant pointer to his political foresight, a quality of the greatest value in a future consort of a sovereign. It enabled Mr. Chuter Ede, the Home Secretary, to reply with complete truthfulness to Mr. George Jeger, M.P., when he asked in the House about priorities for Prince Philip, that he had submitted his application through his commanding officer, in accordance with an arrangement made to give early consideration to applications for naturalisation from foreigners who served during the war in H.M.'s forces.

Together with eight hundred and sixteen others, Prince Philip's naturalisation was announced in the London Gazette of March 18. The announcement, which revealed for the first time that he had renounced his royal titles of Prince and Royal Highness, read: "Mountbatten, Philip: Greece: serving officer in His Majesty's forces; 16 Chester Street, London, S.W.1. 28, February, 1947." Sixteen Chester Street was the town house of Viscount and Viscountess Mountbatten, and Philip's permanent address.

Though his grandfather, Prince Louis of Battenberg, did not renounce his titles on naturalisation as a British subject in 1868, his grandson obeyed the exact letter of King George V's edict in 1932, which ruled that the use of foreign titles by British subjects should be discontinued. He had, as Prince of Greece and Denmark, no surname, for the Royal Family of Denmark is one of those very ancient Sovereign Houses of Europe which carry no patronymic, being listed in the "Almanach de Gotha" as the House of Schleswig-Holstein-Sonderburg-Glucksburg. As a commoner, a surname became a necessity, and it surprised no one that Philip chose the name of the man who had for so many years acted as a father to him, and signed himself "Philip Mountbatten".

Princess Andrew of Greece and Denmark (Princess Alice of Battenberg), Lieutenant Mountbatten's mother

In this, personal preference and political sagacity were equally satisfied, for there could be no better name for a man shortly to be allied to the reigning family of Britain than that borne with such fame and lustre by the youngest of the war's Supreme Commanders.

His application was made on the special "Form S" used by serving members of the Forces. It was signed by his Commanding Officer, who had to answer such questions as: "Would you consider him to be of good character and likely to make a good citizen?" "Does he appear to have become assimilated to the British way of life?" Neither of these questions can have caused the slightest difficulty or hesitation. Prince Philip himself had to declare he was of good character, had an adequate knowledge of the English language, was, to the best of his knowledge, financially solvent, and that, were his application granted, he would either continue in the service of the Crown, or reside in His Majesty's Dominions. All that cost him, as it costs all naturalised subjects, a total of £10 2s. 6d., a pound deposit to the Home Office when he made his application, a half-crown fee to the Commissioner of Oaths before whom he took his Oath of Allegiance, and a final fee of nine pounds to the Home Office when the application was granted.

It is interesting to note that Prince Albert was naturalised only a few days before his marriage to Queen Victoria: that his marriage was the specific and only reason for his naturalisation; and that he retained his princely title of Prince Albert of Saxe-Coburg-Gotha all his life.

It was in 1944, when the end of the war seemed in sight, that Prince Philip formally renounced in writing his claims in the line of succession to the Greek Throne, a step he had refrained from taking earlier, while Greece was under German and Italian domination, because, as he told friends, it would look like deserting in the hour of need. But he retained his Royal rank and style until the naturalisation was completed, when he became plain Philip Mountbatten, with his naval rank as a Lieutenant his only prefix and title, a state of affairs that gave rise to no little confusion and caused many a heated argument in the days immediately following his engagement to Princess Elizabeth, for many people, meeting him with the King and Queen and the Princesses, as a full member of the Royal party, addressed him with the "Sir" of Royalty or high rank. Others, conscious that he had relinquished Royal rank, yet chary of calling him "Lieutenant Mountbatten", avoided the issue altogether. The exact forms seem a little obscure, but it could well be argued that the prospective consort of a Princess of the Blood Royal is, by simple courtesy, and of respect for his bride-to-be, entitled to the "Sir" which only the most churlish would deny him.

Another point of confusion arose over the question whether to bow or not. There is no rule that commoners, unless they hold extremely high office, like the Speaker of the House of Commons, are entitled to a bow, yet it scarcely seemed right to the many hundreds who met Philip and shook hands with him on the Scottish visit, to bow or curtsy to the four other member of the party, and give him a mere handshake. Most people compromised with a quick nod of the head which might be regarded as a bow or not, as you wished, and Princess Margaret, whose sense of the comic is well developed, watched with considerable amusement the indecision of various folk as they left her with an obeisance and went on to meet Philip, whose place was next to her. Nor did Philip himself, quick to note the humour in any situation, fail to appreciate the joke.

Aboard ship, of course, there was no confusion. The Royal Navy is well-used to numbering Princes, both British and foreign, among its officers, and the Service rule is that it is naval rank that counts, so when Lieutenant Philip Mountbatten saluted Admiral Sir Neville Syfret, Commander-in-Chief of the Home Fleet, instead of waiting to return *his* salute, as did the King, he was merely doing exactly what Lieutenant Prince Philip would have done a few months earlier.

CHAPTER SIX

Princess Elizabeth To-day

PRINCESS ELIZABETH has developed greatly in the year of her majority. Before she went to South Africa, two and a half months before her twenty-first birthday, she was still a young girl on the threshold of womanhood, a girl who had already shown signs of an independent character, a strong will, and a penetrating intelligence, but a girl whose sequestered upbringing left her younger, in many ways, than most girls of her age. The crowded memorable experiences of the great ten-thousand-mile tour of the Union, the vast number of new people whom she met, many of them with outlooks differing greatly from her own, her contact for the first time with the proud and sturdy Afrikaaners, her meetings with the Bantu peoples whose chanted songs she so much admired, the inspiring sight of the wide and limitless horizons of Africa, as the White Train moved across the veldt, above all, perhaps, the new and stimulating vision of the Empire as a great whole which Field Marshal Smuts opened to her as they talked together, all these combined to give her more maturity, to give her, as they gave anyone privileged to share that Royal journey, a deeper, more personal understanding of the conception of the British Commonwealth, an understanding of incalculable value to one whose birth places her at the very centre of it.

When Princess Elizabeth, sitting alone in a not very ornately furnished room at Government House, Cape Town, broadcast to the Empire on her twenty-first birthday, on April 21, 1947, and dedicated her life to the service of the great Imperial family, she spoke from her heart.

"I declare," said the Princess in that firm clear voice that the world has come to know so well, "before you all that my whole life, whether it be long or short, shall be devoted to your service, and the service of our great Imperial family, to which we all belong, but I shall not have strength to carry out this resolution alone unless you join in it with me, as I now invite you to do."

With her exact knowledge and lively sense of history, the Princess recalled the vows taken in more knightly days, and recalled, too, the words of William Pitt. "Most of you have read in the history books the proud saying of William Pitt, that England had saved herself by her exertions and would save Europe by her example. But in our time we may say that the British Empire has saved the world first and now has to save itself after the battle is won. I think that is an even finer thing than was done in the days of Pitt, and it is for us who have grown up in these years of danger and glory to see that it is accomplished in the long years of peace that we all hope stretch ahead.

"There is a motto which has been borne by many of my ancestors, a noble motto —'I serve'.

"Those words were an inspiration to many bygone heirs to the throne when they made their knightly dedication as they came to manhood. I cannot do quite as they did, but through the inventions of science I can do what was not possible for any of them. I can make my dedication with a whole Empire listening. I should like to make that dedication now. It is very simple."

As she spoke her solemn words of dedication, and pledged her life to her father's peoples, perhaps the shades of the bygone Kings heard her vows, and if they did, they surely nodded their crowned heads in approving agreement. Away in England, six thousand long miles distant, one man listened to her words with greater attention than most of her millions of hearers, for the dedication which the Princess was making affected his own future life as well as hers, and, though she could not openly give any sign as yet, both she and he knew that her words bound them both to a mutual life of service.

It was about half-way through the South African tour that those close to the Princess noticed a distinct change in her. At first she had, amid the welter of official engagements, parties, dinners, dances, and sight-seeing trips, seemed a little apart, as though she was not wholly absorbed with the business or the gaity in hand. People ascribed this variously to the change of scene and environment, the change of food, and some to the fact that most of those whom the Princesses met were far older than they. Then almost overnight, she seemed to revert to her old self, gayer and more alert, in every way happier and more cheerful. Looking back, it is possible to surmise that this change may have coincided with the private family decision that the engagement between her and Lieutenant Philip Mountbatten should take place on the Royal Family's return. Certain it is that the Princess, from the day her engagement was announced, has exuded happiness. Watching her walk with such lightsome feet that she seemed to be almost dancing down the long corridors of the ancient Palace of Holyroodhouse, during the visit to Edinburgh which immediately followed the engagement, one high official of the Royal Household, whose kindly manners and unruffled calm come from a deep knowledge of mankind and its ways, remarked that had

Princess Elizabeth making her coming-of-age broadcast

the engagement not been announced, it would have been easy to deduce. "The Princess has that radiant air of happiness that you only see in girls who have just become happily engaged," said he. "It is unmistakable, there is nothing else quite like it."

Unmistakable, too, is the mantle of happiness which both she and Lieutenant Mountbatten wear when they are together, the charming little air of proud proprietorship with which she takes his arm and brings him forward from his place at the rear of the Royal group, the thoughtful tenderness with which he anticipates her wish, and lowers or raises the car window. "This Is My Lovely Day," was by chance the title of the first foxtrot the couple danced together in public after the engagement, and it is a title appropriate to any day they spend together, for each shows, in a different way, how much they enjoy every moment they spend in each other's company.

To have a vast crowd singing "All the Nice Girls Love a Sailor" with every eye fixed on you is no easy experience, and that song of grandma's day became a sort of theme song for the crowds outside Buckingham Palace, for the holidaymakers in the Isle of Arran, for the crowds everywhere in Scotland, whenever they saw the Princess and Philip together. But the young couple seemed just to enjoy the fun. They would stand looking into each other's eyes and smiling for all the world to see they were in love.

Another charming incident was at Galashiels, during the Royal tour of the border towns. The King and Queen, followed by Princess Elizabeth and Princess Margaret, signed the Visitors' Book outside the Town Hall, in full view of the crowds. While her sister was signing, Princess Elizabeth walked over to where Lieutenant Mountbatten was standing, spoke a word or two to him, and gently led him forward to sign his name for the first time with those of the Royal Family. The fact that he signed after his future sister-in-law, Princess Margaret, explains something which puzzled many on that Scottish tour. Lieutenant Mountbatten, attentive as he was to his fiancée at all times, did not walk or stand at her side. Princess Margaret was always between them. This, of course, was as it should be, for at that time, Philip, still unmarried, had no Royal precedence, and took his rightful place after the younger Princess.

Princess Elizabeth and Philip have what many philosophers have declared to be the best recipe of all for a happy life together, a sense of humour that sets them laughing at the same things, so that often in public they will catch each other's eye in a look of understanding at some private joke over which they will laugh together later. Princess Alice, Philip's mother, in one of her rare public utterances about her son, remarked that they share a sense of humour. "When the young people are together they laugh about many things that others don't notice," she said.

On the border tour: the Royal pair at a Guard of Honour inspection

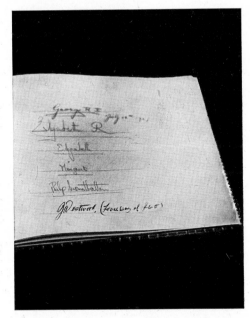

His first signature with the Royal Family: underneath is that of Mr. J. Westwood, Secretary for Scotland

Sampling an orange: a happy study in South Africa

They share, too, the same outlook on life, an outlook of high and serious purpose, combined with an enduring sense of fun. Mountbatten, like most men who have seen active service, is older than his years. He has shown his attitude to life and duty by his years in the Navy, when he shirked no single task, however unpleasant, if it lay in the course of his duties, asked no privileges because of his rank, and claimed no reward for work well done. His appointment as the youngest First Lieutenant of a destroyer in the Service came to him by pure merit, and not on family influence or connections. Lord Louis Mountbatten (as he then was) was given command of the crack destroyer H.M.S. *Kelly* at the beginning of the war because he had proved himself to be the best destroyer officer afloat, not because he was the King's cousin: and so it was with his nephew. The key to Princess Elizabeth's own outlook on her Royal duties is contained in the words of her broadcast quoted at the beginning of this chapter: and the two outlooks spring from the same inner conviction of the duty of doing at all times the best that lies within one's power.

Though Princess Elizabeth's personality has developed so much, she retains the same characteristics that were hers as a young girl, high among them a strong purpose and an ability to get her own way. One of the most recent instances of this was at the Trooping the Colour parade in honour of the King's official birthday this year. As Colonel of the Grenadier Guards, Princess Elizabeth's proper place at this most important of all ceremonial parades of the Brigade of Guards was with the Colonels of the other regiments, at her father's side. But the Colonels ride with

54

PRINCESS ELIZABETH TO-DAY

His Majesty the Colonel-in-Chief, and there was no precedent for Princess Elizabeth appearing on horseback at an official function, nor was there any uniform for her to wear as Colonel. Small difficulties like those serve only to make the Princess more firmly resolved to fulfil her purpose, and long before the Royal party left Africa, she had her father's permission to ride in the Royal procession, and had sent orders to London for suitable designs for a military style tunic and riding habit to be made. It was a habit and not breeches which the Princess ordered in the dark-blue of the Guards officers' undress uniform, for she decided that to ride astride on this occasion would be wrong and out of keeping with the ceremonial nature of the parade. Though she learned to ride side-saddle as a young girl, it was several years since she had practised that elegant style of equitation, so, because it is her way to do everything she does as well as she possibly can, she took a short refresher course in the grounds of Buckingham Palace and at Windsor from a well-known riding mistress. The result was one of those complete successes that leave nothing to be desired. Princess Elizabeth, sitting her big charger with dignity and grace, her figure well set off by her perfectly-cut blue tunic with its shoulder badges of a colonel, a feminine replica of the peaked Guards cap on her thick hair, looked exactly right. Everyone in the crowds who watched the Royal cavalcade ride from the Palace to Horse Guards Parade and back, everyone who saw the young Royal Colonel riding slowly round the statue-still

Rhodesian children of different races combined to give her a twenty-first birthday present: the Princess wears their lily-shaped diamond brooch

ranks of Guardsmen, as her father inspected them, and sitting motionless at his side while the Guards marched past, admired the straightness of her girlish figure, the erect ease with which she sat her horse. Even the King, the epitome of military correctness, his eyes fixed to the front as he returned the salutes of his Guards, must have felt proud as he spared an occasional glance to his side, a pride which the Queen and Queen Mary watching the parade from the traditional place for the Royal ladies, on the balcony of Horse Guards Arch, shared to the full.

The important point about the story is not so much that Princess Elizabeth got her own way, but that her idea proved so right, in spite of the apprehensions expressed beforehand by some of the more senior and conservative-minded officers of the Brigade.

It is another illustration of the fact that the Princess has inherited from her father and her grandfather that gift of anticipating and correctly interpreting public reaction which is so excellent a possession for a constitutional monarch.

In South Africa, Princess Elizabeth showed she possesses another rare gift, of equal importance for one in her position, that of being able to ward off unexpected and embarrassing questions without giving offence. It was a well-meaning and fatherly old Afrikaan farmer holding an official position who, quite early in the tour, asked her straight out the question which nearly everyone in the Empire was wanting to ask:

A hitherto unpublished picture: the three-year-old Princess rides her tricycle in Hamilton Gardens, behind 145 Piccadilly

56

H.R.H. *the Colonel of the Grenadier Guards at the Trooping the Colour Parade on her father's birthday*

"When are you going to become engaged?" The Princess, who might well have been taken aback by this rather brutal and quite unexpected intrusion into her private affairs, realised at once that it was only ignorance of Royal ways which prompted the question. She smiled without the least trace of embarrassment, and answered quietly, "You'll have to wait and see." But the old man was not to be lightly put off. "Won't you have an announcement for us on your birthday?" he asked. Again the Princess smiled, and answered him in the same words as before. Then she turned and left him, for further questions would have amounted to something less than politeness. Those few who watched the incident gave her high praise for her manner of dealing with it. That same necessity for readiness in parrying awkward questions was demonstrated to Lieutenant Mountbatten five months later in Scotland, when a somewhat forceful lady, having been presented to him, immediately asked, "Are you going to get married soon?" Philip smiled, for the actual wedding date was not then settled, and muttered a non-committal reply, which the lady in question later interpreted to eager reporters as a declaration by Philip that the wedding would be on February 11th. Only when they found that date in 1948 would be Ash Wednesday, did the Pressmen realise something was amiss.

It was in Scotland that Princess Elizabeth, in one of the many speeches which she writes herself, revealed a side of her nature which is not generally suspected. She has a poetical mind, and, in a speech in which she declared her great affection for Scotland, she conjured up a vision of a wanderer in a far land, with the pitiless sun beating down, whose thoughts "stray to some well-loved loch with a breeze ruffling its waters, the white clouds sailing overhead, and a curlew crying just out of sight. In bitter weather, the cold seems less unkind as we see in our mind's eye the long

Another birthday present : a casket surmounted with a gold nugget given by the residents of Hartley, S. Rhodesia. The King and Queen examine the gift.

hillside shimmering in the hot sun, with nothing stirring save the bees". Then, when most of her hearers at the lunch tables in the Assembly Rooms, where the Lord Provost was entertaining her after she had received the Freedom of his City, were letting their own minds wander away into some fastness of the Highlands, the Princess showed how much she knows of the orator's art. "You have noticed too that in such dreams the breeze never changes to a cold wind and a driving rain. The bees are there—but never a midge," she said, and the grave dignitaries of Scotland and their ladies laughed long at this sudden descent from Parnassus to the realities of everyday life. Another indication of the Princess's love of poetry is to be found in the number of times quotations find their way into her public speeches. In her twenty-first birthday broadcast, for example, she quoted Rupert Brooke—"Now God be thanked Who has matched us with his hour," and a score of other examples could be added.

The Princess, incidentally, made that important broadcast twice. Once was on her birthday, at Cape Town. The other occasion was a week earlier, while the Royal party were enjoying their only real rest of the tour, amid the peace and natural grandeur of that lovely country that surrounds the Victoria Falls, in Rhodesia. There, the

The Royal couple dance extremely well together at a ball in Scotland

Princess sat in the open, reading her speech in the strong African sunlight, while cinema cameras whirled, camera shutters clicked, and microphones recorded her words. This advance filming and recording was done with a dual purpose. The radio beam from South Africa to London, which would carry the Princess's words on her birthday, is, for certain physical and technical reasons, not entirely reliable. It is liable to sudden and unpredictable breaks, which, should they occur in the midst of her speech, might mean that half the Empire or more might miss large sections of it. To guard against this, the B.B.C., with the sanction of the King and the willing co-operation of the Princess, decided to make a recording which could be flown back to London as a stand-by, for use if radio conditions were bad on the birthday night. If, at the same time, the films and photographs were taken, they, too, could be flown back to London in time for publication on the birthday, instead of a week later. This was done, which explains the slight discrepancy between the newspaper reports which told how the Princess broadcast from a room at Government House, and the pictures which showed her clearly in the open air. But the B.B.C. recordings did not have to be used. The still uncertain factors that govern radio communications were favourable on the night of April 21st, and to her own satisfaction it was the Princess's "live" voice—to use the expressive radio phrase—and not a recording which listeners all over the world heard on her birthday.

Fascinated yet horrified : the Royal visitors watch Johannes handling deadly snakes at Port Elizabeth

A morning canter with Princess Margaret: on the sands at Port Elizabeth

Another story concerning the B.B.C. is worth recounting. On the evening of the day the Royal engagement had been made public, there was a big crowd waiting outside Buckingham Palace in the hope of seeing the betrothed couple. From time to time shouts of "We want Elizabeth, we want Philip" went up. On the steps of the Victoria Memorial a group of cameramen with long focus lenses waiting patiently. Earlier, in the rain of the afternoon, the Queen herself, thoughtful as always of others, had sent out a message telling them there would be no balcony appearances before dinner, and the photographers had gratefully retreated to shelter, to resume their vigil later. On a mobile broadcast van, a B.B.C. commentator kept vigil too, and when his cue came in the middle of the nine o'clock news, he went on the air with nothing to report except the presence of the crowds. While he was doing his best to fill in time, what he and the cameramen and the crowds had all been awaiting happened. The Palace windows were opened, and Princess Elizabeth and her fiancé stepped out onto the balcony, followed by the King and Queen and Princess Margaret. Cheers broke from the crowds, the camera shutters worked, and the B.B.C. man was exultant at the supremely lucky timing of his broadcast, so lucky that it seemed as if it must have been stage-managed. But it was neither luck nor stage-management which brought the Royal couple and the others so opportunely onto the balcony. Princess Elizabeth, listening to the nine o'clock news inside the Palace, heard the commentator filling in time, and knew that was the moment to go out. It was yet another example of her instinctive sense of what to do and the right time to do it.

Since her birthday, Princess Elizabeth has taken on many new duties and has had many new distinctions bestowed upon her. But she is constant to her original rule not to take on more official appointments than she can deal with adequately and properly, and it is only after the most careful consideration to ensure that she will have time to take personal interest in its activities that she consents to any of the many requests which reach her to associate herself with societies and institutions of all kinds. On her birthday, the King appointed her Colonel-in-Chief of the Argyll and Sutherland Highlanders, and of the 16th/5th Lancers.

With the personnel and history of these regiments the Royal Colonel has made herself familiar, as she did in the case of her first military appointment as Colonel of the Grenadier Guards. Next in importance is her Fellowship of the Royal Society, which she took up by right, as a member of the Royal House, on July 3, 1947. Papers from the "Society for the extending of natural knowledge", which was founded by her own ancestor Charles II, have since then been sent to her at the Palace. She has also accepted a diploma of honorary membership of the Institution of Civil Engineers, the Grand Mastership of the Guild of Air Pilots and Navigators, membership of the Worshipful Company of Drapers (to which she was entitled, by patrimony, for the King was also Master) and has become patron of the British Travel Association and President of the Royal Society of Arts. In the King's Birthday Honours, she and her sister Princess Margaret were both appointed to the Imperial Order of the Crown of India—almost certainly the last appointment to that Order—and on July 10, the day of her engagement announcement, the King made her a Dame Grand Cross of the Order of St. John of Jerusalem. She is a Freeman of the City of London, an honour bestowed on her at Guildhall on June 11 with all the traditional pomp and dignified ceremonial for which the City is renowned. This honour, the Princess declared, gave her particular pride, since she is by birth a Londoner: and it was, too, an honour she could claim by patrimony, since her father is also a Freeman of his own capital City. Windsor, the Royal Borough

The King and his daughter watch the waters at Victoria Falls, one of the world's most wonderful sights

beside the Thames, proud of the fact that King George V took its name as the designation of his Royal House, and conscious of its long, close and intimate connections with the Royal Family, also asked the Princess to accept the Freedom of the borough, which she, who spent so much of her girlhood within its boundaries during the war years, gladly did, enjoying the contrast between the friendly, homely atmosphere of the open-air ceremony in Windsor Home Park, and the more elaborate, formal ritual of the earlier freedom ceremony in Guildhall.

To deal with all these new calls on her time, and the many many more which were to follow, it became necessary for the Princess to expand her personal staff, and for the important post of secretary she chose a young man with a brilliant record and long family connections with the Court. He is Mr. "Jock" Colville, whose mother, Lady Cynthia Colville, has been Woman of the Bedchamber and close friend to Queen Mary for more than twenty years. From the Foreign Office, Mr. Colville was picked by Mr. Churchill to join his war-time staff, from which he went into the Royal Air Force, to return to the Foreign Office when peace came. As a married woman, the Princess will make further appointments to her Household in due course.

But, as they planned the start of their married life together, Princess Elizabeth and Lieutenant Mountbatten, like thousands of other post-war married couples, had no house in London of their own. It would have been possible for one of the houses in St. James's or Kensington Palace, which are in the King's gift, to have been repaired, modernised and re-decorated for them. But that would have meant the diversion of much labour and the use of much scarce materials, needed for more urgent housing work. So it was decided, with the full concurrence of the Princess and her fiancé, that for the time being they should make their home at Buckingham Palace. While the first preparations for the wedding were still in progress at Westminster Abbey, while the Lord Chamberlain and his hard pressed staff were still consulting files and looking up precedents before the real business of allotting tickets and dispatching invitations came upon them, two rooms adjoining the small self-contained suite on the second floor which Princess Elizabeth had had as her own for three years past, were being got ready for her husband. That is all that could be done to prepare a London home for the Heiress of England and her bridegroom, a sad reflection, if you like, of the austerity of these our times: but at the same time an inspiring example of the way in which the British Royal Family share in every way the lives of the King's peoples. The simplicity of a suite of half a dozen rooms as their town home fits in, too, with the tastes of both Princess Elizabeth and Philip, for both are people who dislike ostentatious

The Royal pair pay a call: arriving at the Argyll and Sutherland Highlanders Club in Edinburgh

luxury. Mountbatten himself was well used to much less commodious quarters before his marriage. The hut in which he lived at Corsham, one of the group of temporary wartime structures built with little regard for comfort, was no different from those of his brother officers, nor was it more elaborately furnished: and before that he had the cramped quarters of a warship as his abiding place. For her country home, the King gave Princess Elizabeth Sunninghill Park near Ascot, but because of the labour and materials shortage only a few rooms were made ready for the royal couple. Unfortunately the house was gutted by fire some three months before the wedding.

From Buckingham Palace, the Royal couple may go far afield in the days that lie before them. If circumstances dictate that Lieutenant Mountbatten must relinquish his naval career, he is unlikely to be content to live a life of semi-retirement, merely escorting the Princess on her public visits. He has too dynamic a personality, too energetic a mind for that. From Australia, before the engagement, came a suggestion that the King should appoint Princess Elizabeth Governor-General of the great Commonwealth, and there is no constitutional reason why she, or possibly her husband, should not undertake that office in Australia or any other part of the Commonwealth. The whole Empire has been wanting to see Princess Elizabeth for a long time: and the desire is even greater now that the Princess is no longer alone. Princess Elizabeth herself has made no secret of her desire to see as many parts of the Empire of which she may one day be the head. "Before I am much older, I hope I shall come to know many of them," said the Princess, speaking of the homes of the Commonwealth that are to be found in every continent on the earth, and she has a way of making her hopes come true. Where she and her sailor husband may travel cannot be told. But it is certain that wherever they go they will be happy if they are together, for theirs is a true love match: and this small account of the lives of a real Princess of the twentieth century and her princely consort may fittingly end with the words that rounded off the fairy tales of Princesses of a younger day, that they "may live happily ever after".